When Gods Walked Among Us

RAJNISH KUMAR

This is a work of retelling and interpretation. While the stories are based on Hindu mythology and traditional narratives, they have been adapted and simplified for modern readers. The author has made every effort to honor the cultural and spiritual essence of the original tales.

For permissions, rights, or inquiries, please contact:

ISBN Number: 978-93-343-5107-1

First printing edition 2025

Front cover image by - RAJNISH KUMAR

Book design by – RAJNISH KUMAR

Dedication

This book is lovingly dedicated—
To my cherished family, whose unwavering presence transforms every moment and emotion into a tapestry of meaning and joy.

To Kalo, that gentle, voiceless soul whose quiet companionship kindled within me a deeper well of compassion, sensitivity, and connection. In her innocent gaze, I glimpsed the purest essence of life and the boundless depths of love.

And to you—
yes, you— my steadfast companion through every doubt and dream, who helped weave my thoughts into words and shaping this book into a heartfelt offering to the divine legacy of Hindu Religion.

Without each of you, this sacred journey would not have found its voice. — **Rajnish Kumar**

Preface

In every corner of India, faith breathes through the stones of ancient temples, the tales whispered by grandmothers, and the chants that echo through morning aartis. The spirit of devotion has shaped not just our beliefs but our culture, values, and collective consciousness. This book is a humble attempt to explore that rich spiritual heritage through timeless stories of divine beings and sacred places that continue to inspire millions.

Each chapter invites the reader into a different realm—be it the battlefield of wisdom where Lord Murugan leads with courage, the mystical shadows of Patala where Ahiravana lingers, or the compassionate aura surrounding Goddess Yellamma. From the eternal love of Kamadeva and Rati to the might of Kaal Bhairav and the abundant blessings of Lord Kubera, these narratives are not just mythological; they are deeply emotional, symbolic, and transformative.

This book does not merely recount legends; it aims to bridge the gap between devotion and understanding. Whether you are a spiritual seeker, a lover of folklore, or someone curious about India's divine traditions, may these stories serve as a light on your path.

Let the journey begin.

About the Author

Rajnish Kumar is a storyteller, spiritual thinker, and cultural enthusiast with a deep passion for Indian mythology and devotional heritage. His work reflects a lifelong exploration of India's sacred narratives and a commitment to preserving and presenting them in an accessible, heartfelt manner.

Blending research with reverence, Rajnish crafts stories that resonate with modern readers while staying true to their divine essence. Through his writings, he invites readers to see mythology not as distant legends, but as living truths that continue to shape our identity, values, and inner worlds.

When he's not writing, Rajnish can often be found visiting temples, engaging in satsangs, or guiding youth toward a more rooted, conscious connection with Indian culture.

- RAJNISH KUMAR

https://sanskarsarovar.blogspot.com/

puruji.rk@gmail.com

+91-9855103353

Index

Intentionly
Left Blank

The Story of Khatu Shyam Ji

In the heart of Rajasthan, where the golden sands of the desert meet the azure sky, lies a small village called Khatoo, nestled in the Sikar district. Here, a magnificent temple of white Makrana marble stands as a beacon of faith, drawing millions of devotees from across the world. This is the sacred abode of Khatu Shyam Ji, lovingly called Baba Shyam, the deity of the Kali Yuga, the supporter of the defeated, and the granter of heartfelt wishes. His story is not just a tale of valor and sacrifice; it is a saga of devotion, humility, and divine grace that echoes through the ages, rooted in the timeless epic of the Mahabharata.

To the common man, Baba Shyam is more than a god—he is a friend, a guide, a protector who listens to the prayers of the broken and the hopeful alike. His name is chanted with fervor: *"Haare ka Sahara, Baba Shyam Hamara"*—the supporter of the defeated, our beloved Shyam. But who is this divine figure? How did a warrior from the ancient battlefield of Kurukshetra become the revered deity of millions in the modern age? Let us journey back to the time of the Mahabharata, to unravel the extraordinary tale of Barbarika, the mighty warrior who became Khatu Shyam Ji, and discover why his sacrifice continues to inspire hearts even today.

Long ago, in the Dwapar Yuga, when gods and mortals walked the earth together, the land of Bharat was preparing for a great war that would reshape its destiny. This was the time of the Mahabharata, an epic struggle between righteousness and unrighteousness, between the Pandavas and the Kauravas. Amidst this turbulent era, a child was born who would leave an indelible mark on history—not through conquest, but through sacrifice.

In the dense forests of the Kamyaka region, where the Pandavas often sought refuge during their exile, lived Ghatotkacha, the mighty son of Bhima, the second Pandava, and Hidimba, a demoness who had forsaken her violent ways for love. Ghatotkacha was a warrior of immense strength, inheriting the valor of his father and the mystical prowess of his mother's lineage. He married a Naga princess named Ahilawati, also known as Kamkantakata or Morvi in some tales, whose beauty was matched only by her wisdom and courage.

To this extraordinary couple was born a son, a child destined for greatness. They named him Barbarika, inspired by the curly, lion-like locks that adorned his head at birth, resembling the mane of a *babbar sher* (lion). From the moment he opened his eyes, it was clear that Barbarika was no ordinary child. His gaze held a spark of divinity, his strength was uncanny, and his spirit was unyielding. The villagers whispered that he was born with the blessings of the gods, a warrior whose potential could rival even the mightiest heroes of the age.

Barbarika's mother, Ahilawati, was his first teacher. She recognized his extraordinary gifts and began training him in the art of warfare. Under her guidance, Barbarika mastered archery, swordsmanship, and the secrets of mystical combat. His skill was unparalleled, his movements swift and precise, as if the wind itself guided his arrows. But what set Barbarika apart was not just his strength—it was his heart. Even as a child, he was humble, compassionate, and fiercely devoted to justice. He believed that power should serve the weak, and his resolve to protect the downtrodden earned him the love of all who knew him.

As Barbarika grew, his reputation spread beyond the forests. Sages and warriors spoke of a young prodigy whose arrows never missed their mark, whose courage knew no bounds. Yet, the gods had greater plans for him. One day, while meditating in a secluded grove, Barbarika caught the attention of Lord Shiva, the destroyer and the granter of boons. Pleased with the boy's devotion and discipline, Shiva appeared before him in a radiant form, his trident gleaming under the moonlight.

"Barbarika," Shiva's voice rumbled like thunder, "your heart is pure, and your skill is unmatched. I grant you three infallible arrows, known as the *Teen Baan*. With these, you shall be invincible in the three worlds. But use them wisely, for power without purpose is a curse."

Barbarika bowed, his heart swelling with gratitude. The three arrows were no ordinary weapons. The first could mark all targets he wished to destroy, the second could spare those he wished to protect, and the third could execute his will with unerring precision. With these arrows and a divine bow gifted by Agni, the fire god, Barbarika became a force to be reckoned with—a warrior who could single-handedly alter the course of any battle.

Yet, Barbarika's heart remained untouched by pride. He vowed to use his gifts only for the cause of righteousness, to stand by those who needed him most. Little did he know that his vow would soon be tested on the grandest stage of all—the battlefield of Kurukshetra.

The winds of war were sweeping across Bharat. The Pandavas, led by the righteous Yudhishthira, and the Kauravas, driven by Duryodhana's ambition, were preparing for a cataclysmic clash at Kurukshetra. The news of the impending war reached every corner of the land, stirring the hearts of warriors and kings. Barbarika, now a young man, heard of the great battle and felt a fire ignite within him. He was a warrior, born to fight for justice, and the Mahabharata war was the ultimate test of his ideals.

"Mother," Barbarika said one evening, as they sat under the stars, "the war at Kurukshetra will decide the fate of Dharma. I cannot stand by and watch. I must go and witness this great battle."

Ahilawati's heart sank. She knew her son's strength, but she also knew the dangers of war. "My son," she said, her voice trembling, "you are no mere spectator. Your heart will not let you stand on the sidelines. If you join the battle, you will fight, and your power could change everything. Promise me you will choose wisely."

Barbarika smiled, his eyes reflecting the starlight. "I promise, Mother. I will fight only for the side that is just. If I must fight, I will stand with the weaker side, the one that needs my strength to uphold Dharma."

With his mother's blessings and the three infallible arrows in his quiver, Barbarika mounted his blue horse, a gift from his Naga lineage, and set out for Kurukshetra. His heart was resolute, his purpose clear. He would not fight for glory or conquest but for justice, to ensure that righteousness prevailed.

As he journeyed toward the battlefield, Barbarika's path crossed with two mysterious figures disguised as sages. They were none other than Lord Krishna and Arjuna, the Pandava archer, traveling incognito to scout for great warriors who might join the war. Krishna, with his divine wisdom, had heard of Barbarika's prowess and wished to test him.

"Young warrior," Krishna called out, his voice gentle yet commanding, "where are you headed with such a mighty bow and only three arrows?"

Barbarika dismounted and bowed respectfully. "I am Barbarika, son of Ghatotkacha. I go to Kurukshetra to witness the great war. These three arrows are all I need, for they are blessed by Lord Shiva himself."

Krishna's eyes twinkled with curiosity. "Three arrows? Can they match the might of a thousand? Prove your skill, young one."

Barbarika pointed to a nearby peepal tree, its countless leaves rustling in the breeze. "Watch closely," he said. He nocked an arrow, whispered a prayer, and released it. In an instant, the arrow pierced every leaf on the tree, leaving a tiny hole in each one. To Krishna's astonishment, it even pierced a leaf hidden beneath his foot, which he had placed there as a test.

Krishna and Arjuna exchanged glances. This was no ordinary warrior. His skill was divine, his power unmatched. But Krishna, the divine strategist, saw something else—a potential threat to the delicate balance of the war. Barbarika's vow to fight for the weaker side meant he would shift allegiance whenever one side gained the upper hand, prolonging the battle endlessly and potentially annihilating both armies.

"Who will you fight for in this war?" Krishna asked, his tone probing.

"I will fight for the side that is losing," Barbarika replied firmly. "It is my duty to protect the weak and uphold justice."

Krishna's heart stirred with both admiration and concern. Barbarika's intentions were noble, but his power could disrupt the cosmic order. The Kauravas, led by the unrighteous Duryodhana, were destined to lose, for their cause was rooted in greed and adharma. If Barbarika joined them, the Pandavas, champions of righteousness, might face defeat. Yet, Krishna could not deny the purity of Barbarika's heart. He decided to test him further, not with weapons, but with wisdom.

Krishna, still disguised as a sage, smiled warmly at Barbarika. "Your skill is unmatched, young warrior, but true greatness lies not in strength alone. Tell me, are you capable of charity, of giving selflessly for the sake of others?"

Barbarika's eyes shone with conviction. "Ask anything of me, revered sage, and I will give it without hesitation. My life is dedicated to Dharma."

Krishna's gaze softened, but his words carried weight. "Then give me your head, Barbarika. Offer it as charity, for the sake of this war and the greater good."

The request stunned Barbarika. His head? The very essence of his being? Yet, he sensed something divine in the sage's presence. He knelt before Krishna and said, "If my head is what you seek, I offer it willingly. But first, reveal your true form, for I know you are no ordinary sage."

Krishna smiled, and in an instant, his disguise melted away. Before Barbarika stood the dark-skinned, flute-playing Lord of Dwarka, his eyes radiating infinite compassion. Arjuna, too, revealed himself, bowing to his divine cousin. Barbarika fell to his knees, overwhelmed by the presence of Krishna, the incarnation of Vishnu.

"Lord," Barbarika said, his voice steady despite his awe, "why do you ask for my head? If it serves Dharma, I will give it, but tell me the purpose."

Krishna placed a hand on Barbarika's shoulder. "You are a warrior of unparalleled power, Barbarika, but your vow to fight for the losing side could undo the balance of this war. The Kauravas fight for adharma, and their defeat is ordained to restore righteousness. If you join them, the Pandavas, who stand for Dharma, may fall. Your sacrifice is needed not to fight, but to preserve the greater good. Give your head, and I promise you immortality in the hearts of men."

Barbarika's heart swelled with understanding. He saw the wisdom in Krishna's words, the divine plan that transcended his own desires. He had come to Kurukshetra to fight for justice, but now he realized that true justice sometimes demanded surrender, not battle.

"My Lord," Barbarika said, his voice resolute, "I offer my head to you. But grant me one wish: let me witness the Mahabharata war, for it is the greatest battle of our time."

Krishna nodded, his eyes gleaming with pride. "So be it. Your head will watch the war from a hill, and your sacrifice will be remembered for eternity."

With unwavering resolve, Barbarika drew his sword, closed his eyes, and severed his own head, offering it at Krishna's feet. As his lifeblood flowed, a divine light enveloped him, and Krishna blessed the head, ensuring it would remain alive to witness the war. The Pandavas and Krishna carried Barbarika's head to a hill overlooking the Kurukshetra battlefield, where it was placed with reverence. From that vantage point, Barbarika's head would see the epic clash unfold, a silent witness to the triumph of Dharma.

The Mahabharata war raged for eighteen days, a tempest of arrows, swords, and divine weapons that shook the earth. From his hilltop perch, Barbarika's head watched it all—the valor of Arjuna, the strength of Bhima, the cunning of Shakuni, and the tragedy of Karna. But above all, he saw the divine hand of Krishna, guiding the Pandavas with his wisdom and protecting them with his power.

As the war drew to a close, the Pandavas emerged victorious, but a dispute arose among them. Each brother claimed credit for the victory, their egos clashing in the aftermath of battle. Yudhishthira believed his righteousness had won the day, while Arjuna credited his archery, and Bhima his strength. Krishna, ever the peacemaker, smiled and said, "Let us ask the one who saw it all—Barbarika's head."

The Pandavas climbed the hill and stood before the head, which glowed with a divine aura. "Tell us, Barbarika," Yudhishthira asked, "who was the greatest warrior in this war?"

Barbarika's voice, clear and resonant, echoed across the battlefield. "It was Krishna. His Sudarshan Chakra danced through the war, guiding every arrow, shielding every warrior. The Pandavas won because Krishna willed it. Without him, victory would have been impossible."

The Pandavas bowed their heads, humbled by the truth. Krishna, pleased with Barbarika's wisdom, spoke once more. "Your sacrifice has shown the world the power of selflessness, Barbarika. In the Kali Yuga, the age of darkness, you shall be worshipped as Shyam, a form of me. Those who call upon you with a pure heart will have their wishes fulfilled, their troubles erased. You will be the supporter of the defeated, the light in their darkness."

With these words, Krishna immersed Barbarika's head in the Rupawati River, promising that it would resurface in the Kali Yuga to guide humanity. The Pandavas returned to their kingdom, and the story of Barbarika's sacrifice became a legend, whispered among sages and devotees, waiting for the right moment to rekindle faith in a new age.

Centuries passed, and the Dwapar Yuga gave way to the Kali Yuga, an age marked by moral decline and spiritual challenges. The world grew darker, but the promise of Krishna endured. In the village of Khatoo, in what is now Rajasthan, a strange phenomenon began to unfold. A cow, grazing near a sacred pond called Shyam Kund, would stop at a particular spot every day and release milk from her udders, as if offering it to the earth. The villagers, puzzled by this miracle, gathered around the spot and began to dig.

To their astonishment, they uncovered a divine head, glowing with celestial light. It was Barbarika's head, preserved by Krishna's blessing, radiant with divine energy. The villagers, filled with awe, handed the head to Roop Singh Chauhan, the king of Khatoo, and his wife, Narmada Kanwar. That night, the king had a dream in which a divine figure instructed him to build a temple and enshrine the head as Khatu Shyam Ji, the deity of the Kali Yuga.

In 1027 CE, Roop Singh Chauhan constructed the first temple, a modest yet sacred structure, and installed Barbarika's head as the idol of Khatu Shyam Ji. The temple became a place of pilgrimage, drawing devotees who believed that Shyam Baba could fulfill their deepest desires. Over time, the temple was renovated, most notably in 1720 CE by Abhay Singh, who rebuilt it in the grand Makrana marble that stands today. Despite challenges, including an attempt by Mughal emperor Aurangzeb to destroy the temple, the faith of the devotees prevailed, and the worship of Khatu Shyam Ji grew stronger.

The temple became a symbol of hope, a place where the broken-hearted found solace, and the defeated found strength. Devotees began to call him *Lakhdatar* (the giver of millions) and *Teen Baan Dhari* (the wielder of three arrows), honoring his miraculous powers and his legendary past. The Phalgun Mela, a grand festival held in the Hindu month of Phalguna (February-March), became the heart of devotion, attracting lakhs of pilgrims who carried saffron flags in the Nishaan Yatra, chanting *"Jai Shri Shyam"* as they walked to the temple.

The fame of Khatu Shyam Ji spread far and wide, not just in Rajasthan but across India and beyond. Devotees believed that chanting *"Jai Shri Shyam"* or offering a thread at the temple could bring divine intervention. The Shyam Kund, where Barbarika's head was found, became a sacred site, with pilgrims taking dips to heal their ailments and seek blessings. The temple's five daily aartis—Mangala, Shringaar, Bhog, Sandhya, and Sayana—filled the air with devotion, as the idol of Shyam Baba, adorned with flowers and silver ornaments, radiated divine love.

Beyond the miracles, the story of Khatu Shyam Ji carries profound lessons for humanity. Barbarika's life teaches us that true strength lies in sacrifice, not conquest. His willingness to give his head for the greater good reflects the importance of selflessness in the face of personal ambition. His vow to support the weaker side reminds us to stand by those who are struggling, to be a beacon of hope in their darkest moments.

Krishna's blessing to Barbarika underscores the power of devotion. In the Kali Yuga, where distractions and moral challenges abound, Shyam Baba teaches us to surrender our ego to the divine, to trust in the greater plan. His mantra, *"Jai Shri Shyam,"* is a call to simplicity—faith does not require grand gestures but a pure heart. The act of tying a thread or offering a flag at the temple symbolizes surrender, a reminder that true victory lies in humility.

The story also reflects the interplay of karma and destiny. Barbarika's past life as a Yaksha, cursed for his arrogance, shows that every action has consequences, but redemption is always possible through sacrifice and devotion. His transformation into Shyam Ji illustrates that even in the darkest age, divine grace is accessible to those who seek it with sincerity.

Today, the Khatu Shyam Ji Temple stands as a testament to the enduring power of faith. Its white marble spires gleam under the Rajasthan sun, welcoming all who come with a prayer in their hearts. The Phalgun Mela, with its vibrant processions and saffron flags, is a celebration of Barbarika's sacrifice, a reminder that even in the Kali Yuga, hope and compassion prevail.

For the common man, Shyam Baba is a friend who listens, a protector who uplifts, and a guide who leads. His story is not confined to the pages of the Mahabharata or the walls of a temple—it lives in the hearts of millions who chant his name, tie a thread, or take a dip in the Shyam Kund. Whether it is a farmer seeking rain, a student praying for success, or a mother hoping for her child's health, Shyam Baba hears them all.

As we stand before his idol, adorned with garlands and turbans, we are reminded of a warrior who gave everything for Dharma, a deity who became the supporter of the defeated. His story teaches us that sacrifice is not a loss but a legacy, that devotion is not a ritual but a way of life. In the words of his devotees: *"Jako Rakhe Shyam, Maar Sake Na Koi"*—he whom Shyam protects, none can harm.

And so, the saga of Khatu Shyam Ji continues, a flame of faith that burns bright in the Kali Yuga, guiding us through the darkness with the promise of divine love.

The Divine: Salasar Balaji

In the heart of Rajasthan, where the golden sands stretch endlessly under the blazing sun, lies a small town called Salasar in the Churu district. Here, amidst the arid landscape, stands a temple that radiates divine energy, drawing millions of devotees from across India and beyond. This is the Salasar Balaji Temple, a sacred shrine dedicated to Lord Hanuman, the monkey god and eternal devotee of Lord Rama. Known as Salasar Dham, it is a place where wishes are fulfilled, hearts find peace, and faith transforms lives.

To the common man, Salasar Balaji is more than a temple—it is a sanctuary of hope, a place where the impossible becomes possible through devotion. The idol of Hanuman here, adorned with a beard, mustache, and a tilak on his forehead, is unlike any other in India, its uniqueness a testament to the divine miracles that surround its origin. Devotees call him *Balaji*, a name that echoes with reverence, and they flock to his temple to tie coconuts, offer churma, and chant his name, believing that their prayers will reach the heavens.

But how did this humble village become a global pilgrimage site? What is the story behind the swayambhu (self-manifested) idol of Hanuman that draws lakhs of devotees every year? Let us embark on a journey through time, to the dusty fields of 18th-century Rajasthan, to uncover the history, myths, and spiritual significance of Salasar Balaji, a place where faith and miracles intertwine.

Our story begins in the year 1754 CE, in a small village called Asota in Rajasthan's Nagaur district. The land was rugged, the people simple, and life revolved around the rhythms of farming and faith. In this village lived a Ginthala Jat farmer named Dangarmal, a hardworking man who tilled his fields with devotion to both the earth and the divine. One Saturday, on the ninth day of the bright half of the Shravana month (Shravana Shukla Navami, Samvat 1811), Dangarmal set out to plough his field as he did every day. The sun was high, the air thick with heat, and the soil crunched under his plough.

As he guided his oxen, the plough suddenly struck something hard, halting his work with a jolt. A strange, resonant sound echoed from the ground, like a bell struck in a temple. Curious, Dangarmal knelt down and brushed away the sand, expecting to find a rock. Instead, his fingers uncovered a stone idol, its surface smooth and radiating a faint glow. As he cleared more earth, he saw the figure of Lord Hanuman, but not as he had ever seen him before. This Hanuman had a round face, a beard, and a mustache, with knotty eyebrows and compassionate eyes framed by a sacred tilak. It was a sight both majestic and mysterious, unlike any idol in the land.

Dangarmal's heart raced with awe and fear. He called out to his wife, who was bringing his lunch of bajra churma, a simple dish made of crushed pearl millet, ghee, and jaggery. Together, they gazed at the idol, their hands trembling with reverence. Without hesitation, Dangarmal offered the churma to the idol, a humble act of devotion that would become a sacred tradition. The news of the discovery spread like wildfire through Asota, drawing villagers to the field. They whispered among themselves, sensing that something divine had touched their lives.

That night, two extraordinary events unfolded. The Thakur of Asota, the local landlord, had a vivid dream. Lord Hanuman appeared before him, his form radiant and commanding, and said, “The idol you have found is my swayambhu form, a gift to my devotees. Take it to Salasar, where it is destined to be enshrined. Build a temple there, and I will bless all who come with faith.” At the same time, in the distant village of Salasar, a devout Brahmin named Mohandas Maharaj, known for his deep devotion to Hanuman, had a similar dream. Hanuman instructed him to receive the idol from Asota and consecrate it in Salasar, promising that it would become a beacon of faith for generations.

The next morning, the Thakur of Asota woke with a sense of purpose. He summoned the villagers and shared his dream, only to learn that Mohandas had sent a message from Salasar, describing the same divine vision without ever visiting Asota. The coincidence was nothing short of a miracle, and the villagers knew they were part of a divine plan. The Thakur decided to honor Hanuman’s command. He placed the idol in a bullock cart, driven by two bulls, and declared that the temple would be built wherever the cart stopped. With songs of praise and beating drums, the

villagers accompanied the cart as it journeyed toward Salasar, their hearts filled with joy.
In Salasar, Mohandas awaited the idol's arrival. A man of saintly disposition, Mohandas had been born in Rulyani village, Sikar district, to Pandit Lacchiram Patodia. From childhood, he was drawn to devotion, spending hours in prayer and satsang (spiritual gatherings). Astrologers had predicted at his birth that he would become a radiant saint, and his life seemed to fulfill that prophecy. After his sister Kanhi, widowed and living in Salasar with her son Uday, called for his help, Mohandas moved to the village, where his devotion to Hanuman grew even deeper.
When the bullock cart reached Salasar, it stopped abruptly at a spot near the village's edge, refusing to move further despite the efforts of the drivers. The villagers saw this as a sign from Hanuman himself. Mohandas, tears streaming down his face, welcomed the idol with prayers and offerings. With the help of two Muslim artisans, Noora and Dau from Fatehpur Shekhawati, he began constructing a modest mud-stone temple in 1755 CE. This act of unity, with Hindus and Muslims working together, set a timeless example of harmony and devotion. By 1759 CE, the temple was complete, and the idol was enshrined with great ceremony, marking the birth of Salasar Balaji Dham.

The Salasar Balaji Temple, though simple in its beginnings, soon became a magnet for devotees. The idol's unique appearance—Hanuman with a beard and mustache, a form unseen elsewhere in India—drew curiosity and reverence. Mohandas, now revered as a saint, dedicated his life to serving Balaji. He adorned the idol with ghee and vermillion, and legend has it that during one such act of devotion, the idol transformed, taking on the powerful form seen today, as if Hanuman himself had reshaped it to reflect his divine will.

Mohandas's devotion was legendary. He would lose himself in chanting the Hanuman Chalisa, his voice echoing through the temple. One day, while suffering from severe stomach pain, he prayed fervently before the idol. His wife, understanding his pain, offered prayers on his behalf, and miraculously, Mohandas was healed. This event strengthened the belief that Salasar Balaji was a living deity, capable of performing miracles for those who surrendered to him.

In 1759 CE, Mohandas entrusted the temple's care to his disciple, Pandit Udairam, and his descendants, passing on his sacred robe as a symbol of responsibility. In 1794 CE, on the 13th day of the bright half of Baisakh (Baisakh Shukla Trayodashi), Mohandas entered Jeevit Samadhi, consciously leaving his body to merge with the divine. His legacy lived on, and the temple grew in stature, drawing devotees from Rajasthan, Haryana, Punjab, and beyond.

Over time, the mud-stone structure was transformed into a grand edifice. In the early 19th century, Rao Devi Singh, the successor of Sikar's Jagirdar, renovated the temple, using bricks, lime, cement, and white Makrana marble. The sanctum sanctorum (garbha griha) and prayer hall (sabha mandap) were adorned with intricate gold and silver work, while the entrance gates and ritual utensils were crafted from silver. The parikrama path, where devotees circumambulate the shrine, was laid with marble, its floral patterns shimmering under the desert sun. The construction, completed over two years, gave the temple its present-day splendor, a blend of simplicity and magnificence that reflects Hanuman's strength and humility.

The temple became known as a Shakti Sthal, a place of divine power, and a swayambhu shrine, where the idol's self-manifestation was seen as a miracle. Devotees believed that Balaji fulfilled their wishes, healed their ailments, and protected them from misfortune. The temple's fame spread, and by the 20th century, it was a cornerstone of Rajasthan's spiritual landscape, part of a sacred trio alongside the Khatu Shyam Ji Temple and the Rani Sati Temple in Jhunjhunu.

The Salasar Balaji Temple is alive with devotion, its air filled with the sound of bells, bhajans, and the rhythmic chants of the Hanuman Chalisa. The temple opens at 4:00 AM, when priests perform the Mangala Aarti, a serene ritual that awakens the deity with offerings of light and song. Throughout the day, devotees throng the shrine, participating in aartis like the Shringaar Aarti, Bhog Aarti, Sandhya Aarti at 7:10 PM, and Shayan Aarti at 10:00 PM. On Tuesdays, a special Rajbhog Mahaprasad Aarti at 10:00

AM draws large crowds, as Tuesday is considered Hanuman's sacred day.

One of the most cherished rituals is the offering of bajra churma, a tradition rooted in Dangarmal's first offering in 1754. Devotees prepare churma with pearl millet, ghee, jaggery, and dried fruits, believing it pleases Balaji and brings his blessings. Another popular practice is the coconut-tying ritual, where devotees wrap a red thread (moli) around a coconut and tie it to a tree or railing in the temple premises. This act, begun by Rao Raja Devi Singh in hopes of having a son, is believed to fulfill heartfelt wishes when done with devotion. Lakhs of coconuts are tied each year, their presence a colorful testament to the faith of Balaji's devotees.

The Savamani ritual is another hallmark of Salasar. Devotees, especially newlyweds or those celebrating joyous occasions, offer 50 kilograms of food—often laddus or other sweets—as prasad to Balaji. This offering is distributed among the poor, reflecting Hanuman's spirit of service. Drinking water from the temple's wells is also considered sacred, believed to carry Balaji's blessings for health and prosperity.

Every Tuesday and Saturday, the temple buzzes with energy, as these days are particularly auspicious for Hanuman worship. The recitation of the Sunderkhand from the Ramcharitmanas, led by 13 Brahmin singers, fills the air with devotion. During these gatherings, devotees chant mantras like the Hanuman Mool Mantra and *Atulita Bala*

Dhaamam, praising Hanuman's infinite strength and devotion to Rama.

The temple's grandest celebrations occur during two annual fairs: Chaitra Purnima (March-April), marking Hanuman Jayanti, and Ashvin Purnima (September-October), known as Sharad Purnima. During these festivals, lakhs of pilgrims flock to Salasar, transforming the town into a sea of devotion. The Chaitra Purnima fair, celebrating Hanuman's birth, is especially vibrant, with processions, bhajans, and kirtans echoing through the streets. Devotees carry flags, sing praises, and offer prayers, their faith uniting them in a shared love for Balaji.

The Salasar Balaji Temple is steeped in myths and stories that amplify its divine aura. One popular legend explains the idol's unique appearance. It is said that when Mohandas first adorned the idol with ghee and vermillion, Hanuman appeared to him in a dream, revealing his bearded and mustached form. Moved by this vision, Mohandas reshaped the idol to reflect what he saw, creating the distinctive image that sets Salasar Balaji apart from other Hanuman temples. Devotees believe this form embodies Hanuman's mature, powerful aspect, a warrior-saint who combines strength with compassion.

Another tale speaks of the temple's origins as a response to a crisis. Centuries ago, the region around Salasar, then known as Gandas ki Dhani, suffered from severe water scarcity due to famines. The discovery of the idol and the establishment of the temple were seen as divine interventions, bringing not only spiritual solace but also prosperity to the region. The wells of Salasar, believed to be blessed by Hanuman, became a source of clean water, and devotees today drink from them, trusting in their healing powers.

The temple is renowned for its miracles, stories of which are shared by devotees with awe and gratitude. One such story tells of a poor widow named Kamla, who lived in a nearby village. Struggling to feed her children, she visited Salasar Balaji during Chaitra Purnima, tying a coconut with a prayer for sustenance. That night, she dreamt of Hanuman, who assured her of his protection. The next day, a merchant passing through the village offered her a job, and her family never went hungry again. Kamla's story spread, inspiring others to seek Balaji's blessings.

These stories, passed down through generations, have cemented Salasar Balaji's reputation as a place where wishes come true. From barren couples seeking children to students praying for success, devotees believe that Balaji listens to every heartfelt prayer. The coconut-tying ritual, in particular, is seen as a powerful act of faith, with countless stories of fulfilled wishes—from marriages to recoveries—attributed to it.

Salasar Balaji is more than a temple; it is a spiritual haven that embodies the essence of Hanuman's qualities: strength, devotion, and selflessness. In the Ramayana, Hanuman is the ultimate devotee of Lord Rama, serving him with unwavering loyalty and humility. At Salasar, this spirit is palpable. The temple's simplicity, despite its grandeur, reflects Hanuman's humility, while its vibrant rituals mirror his boundless energy.

For devotees, Salasar is a Shakti Sthal, a place where divine energy flows freely. The swayambhu idol is believed to be a living embodiment of Hanuman, responding to the prayers of those who approach with a pure heart. The temple's rituals, from churma offerings to coconut tying, are acts of surrender, teaching devotees to let go of ego and trust in the divine.

The temple also fosters a sense of community and equality. People from all walks of life—rich and poor, Hindu and non-Hindu—come to Salasar, united by their faith in Balaji. The involvement of Muslim artisans in the temple's construction is a powerful reminder of India's syncretic traditions, where devotion transcends religious boundaries. The Shri Hanuman Seva Samiti, which manages the temple, ensures that devotees are welcomed with open arms, providing free lodging in over 125 dharamshalas and food at community kitchens.

In the Kali Yuga, an age marked by spiritual challenges, Salasar Balaji offers a beacon of hope. Hanuman, known as the Sankat Mochan (remover of obstacles), is believed to protect his devotees from adversity. The temple's rituals and festivals reinforce this belief, reminding people that faith can overcome any obstacle. The Hanuman Chalisa, chanted fervently by devotees, is a prayer of strength and surrender, its verses echoing Hanuman's promise to stand by those who call upon him.

Reaching Salasar Balaji is a pilgrimage in itself, a journey that mirrors the spiritual quest for divine connection. Located on National Highway 65, Salasar is accessible by road, rail, and air. From Jaipur, a 3-4 hour drive (180 kilometers) brings pilgrims to the temple, while buses from Delhi, Haryana, and Punjab make regular trips. The nearest railway stations are Sujangarh and Sikar, a short taxi or bus ride away, and Jaipur International Airport, 160 kilometers away, connects Salasar to the world.

The journey is as enriching as the destination. Pilgrims often travel in groups, singing bhajans and sharing stories of Balaji's miracles. The desert landscape, with its stark beauty, sets the stage for introspection, preparing devotees for the spiritual experience awaiting them. During the Chaitra and Ashvin Purnima fairs, the roads to Salasar are alive with color, as devotees carry flags and chant *"Jai Shri Hanuman Ki"*.

The temple's facilities, managed by the Shri Hanuman Seva Samiti, ensure a comfortable visit. Over 125 dharamshalas offer free or affordable lodging, and community kitchens serve simple, sattvic food. The temple's three gates, adorned with marble carvings, welcome devotees, while shoe stands and clear signage make the experience seamless. For those seeking a closer darshan, a VIP queue allows worship near the idol, though the general queue, though longer, is filled with the same devotion.

The Salasar Balaji Temple has not only transformed the spiritual landscape but also the local economy. The influx of pilgrims has created jobs, from priests and artisans to shopkeepers and hoteliers. Small businesses selling coconuts, churma, and devotional items thrive, while restaurants serve Rajasthan's famous dal baati churma alongside prasad. The temple's fairs, especially Hanuman Jayanti, boost tourism, drawing visitors to nearby attractions like the Mata Anjana Devi Temple, dedicated to Hanuman's mother, just 1 kilometer away.

The temple's influence extends beyond Rajasthan. In Haryana, newlyweds visit Salasar to offer Savamani, seeking blessings for a happy marriage. In Punjab and Uttar Pradesh, devotees undertake padayatras (foot pilgrimages) to Salasar, carrying flags and singing bhajans. The temple's live streaming of aartis, introduced in recent years, allows devotees worldwide to participate in its rituals, connecting the global diaspora to Balaji's grace.

The story of Salasar Balaji is a testament to the power of faith. From a farmer's discovery in a field to a global pilgrimage site, the temple embodies Hanuman's promise to protect and uplift. Its rituals, rooted in simplicity, remind us that devotion requires only a pure heart. The coconut tied with a moli, the churma offered with love, the chants of the

Hanuman Chalisa—these are not mere acts but bridges to the divine.

As the sun sets over Salasar, casting a golden glow on the temple's marble spires, the sound of the Sandhya Aarti fills the air. Devotees, their faces alight with faith, raise their hands in prayer, their voices blending in a chorus of devotion. The idol of Salasar Balaji, with its bearded face and compassionate eyes, seems to smile, a silent assurance that every prayer is heard.

For centuries, Salasar Balaji has been a refuge for the weary, a hope for the hopeless, and a light in the darkness. Its story, born in a farmer's field and nurtured by a saint's devotion, is a reminder that the divine is never far from those who seek it. Whether it is a coconut tied with faith, a churma offered with love, or a simple chant of *"Jai Shri Hanuman Ki"*, Balaji responds, his strength and compassion a balm for every soul.

As we leave the temple, carrying the blessings of Balaji in our hearts, we are reminded of Hanuman's eternal vow: to serve, to protect, to uplift. In the Kali Yuga, where challenges abound, Salasar Balaji stands as a sanctuary of hope, a place where miracles are not just stories but lived experiences. For every devotee who walks through its gates, Salasar is not just a destination—it is a homecoming, a return to the divine embrace of Hanuman.

Goddess Yellamma

As the sun rises over the rolling hills of Saundatti in Karnataka or the vibrant streets of Hyderabad in Telangana, a gentle hum of devotion fills the air. Devotees, draped in colorful sarees and carrying baskets of flowers, coconuts, and neem leaves, make their way to the sacred temples of Goddess Yellamma. She is the Mother of the Universe, the compassionate Jagadamba, the protector of the marginalized, and the divine feminine who resonates deeply in the hearts of millions. Her story is not just one of mythology but a tapestry woven with history, faith, rituals, and the unbreakable bond between the goddess and her people.

Yellamma, is known by many names—Renuka, Jogamma, Ellai Amman, and more. Her worship is a vibrant thread in the cultural fabric of South India, especially in Telangana and Karnataka, where her temples stand as beacons of hope and spirituality.

A Divine Birth from the Sacred Fire

The story of Yellamma begins with a spark of divinity, quite literally. According to ancient texts like the Mahabharata, Harivamsa, and Bhagavata Purana, Yellamma, originally named Renuka, was born from a holy fire ritual, a yajna, performed by her father, King Renu (or Renuka Raja), in the Vidarbha region of Maharashtra. This wasn't just any ritual—it was a sacred act to ensure peace, prosperity, and the continuation of the king's lineage. King Renu, a ruler of the Suryavamsha Ikshvaku dynasty, was childless despite having three wives, a source of great sorrow for him. On the advice of his court priests, he performed this powerful yajna, and from the flames emerged a radiant girl, Renuka, believed to be an incarnation of Goddess Parvati herself in the Kruthayuga (the first age in Hindu cosmology).

Renuka was no ordinary child. Bright, active, and filled with divine energy, she was cherished by her parents and the kingdom. By the age of eight, the sage Agastya, a revered spiritual guide, foresaw her destiny and advised King Renu to marry her to the great sage Jamadagni when she came of age. Jamadagni, known for his wisdom and ascetic life, was one of the Saptarishis (seven great sages) and lived a life devoted to spiritual practices. Renuka, with her divine origins, was the perfect match for him, and their union marked the beginning of a story that would echo through the ages.

From Renuka to Yellamma: A Tribal and Universal Goddess

While Renuka's story is rooted in the Sanskrit texts, her transformation into Yellamma, the goddess of the masses, is deeply tied to the pastoral and tribal communities of South India, particularly the Dhangar and Kurumba communities of Karnataka and Maharashtra. These communities, often marginalized, saw in Yellamma a protector and nurturer who understood their struggles. Her name, "Yellamma," meaning "Mother of All" (from "yella" meaning "all" in Kannada and Telugu), reflects her universal appeal. She is also called Jagadamba, the Mother of the Universe, a title that captures her role as a compassionate deity who embraces all, regardless of caste or status.

Historically, the worship of Yellamma can be traced back to the Chalukyan period (6th–12th centuries CE), when her fertility cult gained prominence in the Deccan region. Archaeological evidence, such as potsherds from the 3rd century BCE to the 3rd century CE found near her temple in Saundatti, suggests that her worship predates even the Chalukyas, possibly originating with nomadic tribes who revered her as a goddess of fertility and protection. The Chalukyas, after taking control of the region from the Kadambas of Banavasi, further integrated her worship into the broader Hindu pantheon, linking her to Parashurama, the sixth avatar of Lord Vishnu, and cementing her status as a divine mother.

The Yellamma Temple in Saundatti, built in 1514 by Bomappa Nayaka of Raybag, stands as a testament to her enduring legacy. Perched atop the Siddhachal Parvat (now called Yellamma Gudi), overlooking the Malaprabha River, this temple is one of the most significant pilgrimage sites in Karnataka. Similarly, the Balkampet Yellamma Temple in Hyderabad, Telangana, draws thousands of devotees, especially during the Ashadha month for the Yellamma Kalyanothsavam festival. These temples are not just places of worship but cultural hubs where traditions, stories, and rituals come alive.

Yellamma as a Syncretic Deity

What makes Yellamma unique is her syncretic nature. She is known by many names across regions—Renuka, Ekvira, Mariamma, Pochamma, Holiyamma, and more—each reflecting local traditions and beliefs. In Telangana, she is often worshipped alongside other gramadevatalu (village goddesses) like Pochamma and Maisamma, who protect communities from disease and calamity. In Karnataka, she is revered as Renukambe, particularly in places like Chandragutti, where her temple dates back to the Kadamba period. In Maharashtra, she is Ekvira, the Kuladevata (family deity) of the Koli community. This diversity of names and forms underscores her role as a goddess who transcends boundaries, uniting diverse communities under her maternal care.

Her association with the Devadasi system, a controversial practice where women were dedicated to temple service, also shaped her historical narrative. While the system was outlawed in the 20th century, it was once a significant part of Yellamma's worship, particularly among lower-caste communities. The Devadasis, or Joginis, were seen as sacred women serving the goddess, though their role often led to exploitation, a topic we'll explore later in the modern context.

The stories of Yellamma are as vibrant as the festivals that honor her. They are drawn from ancient texts like the Mahabharata (Anusasanparva and Vanaparva), Puranas

(Brahmandapurana, Vishnupurana, Skandapurana), and regional folklore. Each tale adds a layer to her divine persona, portraying her as a devoted wife, a wronged mother, and a resurrected goddess who triumphs over adversity.

The Myth of Renuka's Beheading

The most well-known story of Yellamma revolves around Renuka, the wife of Sage Jamadagni and mother of Parashurama. Renuka was known for her purity and devotion. Every morning, she would go to the Malaprabha River to fetch water for her husband's rituals. Using her divine powers, she crafted pots from river sand, supported by a snake that coiled around them, and carried the water back to the ashram. Her chastity and focus were so profound that the pots never broke.

One day, while at the river, Renuka saw a group of Gandharvas (celestial beings) or youths playing in the water. Some versions say she was distracted by their beauty, others that she felt a fleeting moment of desire or simply lost her focus. Whatever the reason, her concentration wavered, and the sand pots dissolved. She returned to the ashram empty-handed. Jamadagni, with his sage's intuition, sensed her lapse and was consumed with rage. He ordered his five sons to behead their mother as punishment for her perceived infidelity. Four of them refused, and Jamadagni cursed them to become eunuchs. The fifth son, Parashurama, known for his unwavering obedience, carried out his father's command and beheaded Renuka.

But the story doesn't end in tragedy. Parashurama, granted a boon by his father for his obedience, asked for his mother and brothers to be restored to life. Miraculously, Renuka's spirit multiplied, and her head was said to have scattered across regions, giving rise to her worship in multiple places. In some versions, her head was replaced with that of a lower-caste woman named Yellamma or Matangi, symbolizing the fusion of Brahminical and tribal traditions. This act of resurrection transformed Renuka into Yellamma, the goddess who forgives and protects all, especially the marginalized.

The Miracle of the Multiplied Heads

Another fascinating tale speaks of Renuka's head multiplying "by tens and hundreds" after her beheading, spreading her divine presence across South India. This miracle inspired her sons and followers, including the cursed eunuchs, to worship her. Each head became a focal point of devotion, explaining why Yellamma is worshipped in so many forms and places. In Saundatti, her head is revered, while in Mahur, Maharashtra, her body is said to reside. This story underscores her universal presence and her ability to connect with diverse communities.

The Penance of Renuka

After being cursed by Jamadagni, Renuka wandered east, desolate and seeking redemption. In the forest, she met the saints Eknath and Joginath, who consoled her and guided her toward penance. They instructed her to bathe in a nearby lake, worship a Shivalinga they gave her, and beg for rice in the villages—a ritual called "Joga Bedodu" in Karnataka, "Jogawa" in Marathi, and "Yellamma Jogu" in Telangana. She was to give half the rice to the saints, cook the rest with jaggery, and eat it with devotion. After three days of this ritual, she was allowed to return to her husband. This story highlights Yellamma's resilience and her connection to rituals that are still practiced by her devotees, particularly women, who undertake similar acts of penance and offering.

The Kamadhenu Cow and Renuka's Sati

Another legend links Yellamma to the mythical Kamadhenu cow, a wish-fulfilling divine creature. According to the Devi Gita (a chapter of the Devi Bhagawatam), King Sahasrarjuna (Kartavirya Arjuna) coveted the Kamadhenu cow owned by Jamadagni and Renuka. When they refused to part with it, he killed Jamadagni. In grief, Renuka performed sati, immolating herself on her husband's pyre, either at Mahur, Maharashtra, or in the Renuka Sanctuary in Himachal Pradesh, where a lake bears her name. Her sacrifice elevated her to divine status, and she became a symbol of devotion and sacrifice.

In Telangana, Yellamma is often worshipped as an aniconic deity, represented by a clay altar from a termite hill, smeared with turmeric and vermillion. One local story tells of Yellamma as a goddess who emerged from an anthill ("Renu" means anthill in some interpretations), symbolizing her connection to the earth and fertility. In Karnataka, she is associated with neem leaves, which devotees carry in their mouths during the "Nimmana" ritual, circumambulating her temple. These regional tales emphasize her role as a goddess of the land, revered by agrarian and pastoral communities.

Yellamma is more than a mythological figure; she is a living presence in the lives of her devotees. Her worship is deeply rooted in the belief that she is a compassionate mother who protects the vulnerable, heals the afflicted, and grants fertility and prosperity. Let's explore the core beliefs and the significance of her worship.

The Mother of the Marginalized

Yellamma is often called the "Goddess of the Fallen," a title that reflects her role as a protector of those on the fringes of society—Dalits, Bahujans, and transgender communities. Her story of being wronged and resurrected resonates with those who face injustice or hardship. In Telangana, she is one of the gramadevatalu, village goddesses who guard settlements and ward off diseases like smallpox and measles. Her sister goddesses, like Pochamma and Maisamma, share this role, but Yellamma's prominence is unmatched, especially in rural areas.

Her association with lower-caste communities, particularly the Madiga and other Dalit groups, underscores her inclusivity. Unlike many deities tied to Brahminical traditions, Yellamma's worship is egalitarian, welcoming all who seek her blessings. This inclusivity is evident in the Jogathi community, which includes transgender individuals who perform the ritualistic Jogathi Nruthya (Yellammaanata) dance, singing her legends and seeking alms in her name.

Symbols of Power and Purity

Yellamma's iconography is rich with symbols. The trident (Trishula) represents her power, the lotus her purity, and the ox her connection to agrarian life. In Telangana, she is often worshipped as an aniconic altar, while in Karnataka, her temples house her image, sometimes depicted with neem leaves or a basket of offerings. These symbols reflect her dual nature as a fierce protector (like Kali) and a nurturing mother (like Parvati).

The Devadasi Connection

One of the most complex aspects of Yellamma's worship is her association with the Devadasi system. Historically, young girls from lower-caste families were dedicated to Yellamma as Joginis or Devadasis, serving the temple through rituals, dance, and music. They were seen as "married" to the goddess or her brother, Potharaju, and took vows of celibacy from human marriage, dedicating their lives to her service. These vows included fasting on Tuesdays and Fridays, begging with a metal mask of the goddess (Joga), and serving the poor and needy.

While this practice was rooted in devotion, it often led to exploitation, with some Devadasis being pushed into prostitution. This gave rise to the misconception that Yellamma's worship inherently involves such practices. However, the core belief is that Devadasis were sacred servants of the goddess, embodying her spirit and serving as intermediaries between her and the community. The British colonial government and later Indian laws banned the Devadasi system, but remnants persist in secret, often misunderstood or commercialized.

Healing and Fertility

Yellamma is revered as a healer, particularly for skin diseases. The sacred wells at her temples, like the Jogal Bhavi in Saundatti or the well at Balkampet, are believed to have curative powers. Devotees bathe in these waters, called tirtham, to seek relief from ailments. She is also a goddess of fertility, invoked by childless couples and those seeking prosperity. The Yellamma Jatre, a grand festival in Saundatti, is a time when devotees offer prayers for children, health, and protection from calamity.

The worship of Yellamma is a vibrant blend of rituals, festivals, and community practices that bring her devotees together. These rituals are not just acts of devotion but expressions of a living tradition that connects the past with the present.

The Yellamma Jatre: A Festival of Faith

The Yellamma Jatre, held annually in Saundatti, is the heart of her worship. Thousands of devotees from Karnataka, Telangana, Maharashtra, and Andhra Pradesh gather to honor the goddess. The festival, held during the Ashadha month (June–July) or around December, is marked by vibrant processions, music, and dance. Devotees carry baskets of offerings—flowers, fruits, coconuts, and puffed rice—while chanting mantras like the "Renuka Ashtakam," a hymn praising her virtues.

One of the most striking rituals is the "Nimmana," where devotees circumambulate the temple with neem leaves in their mouths, symbolizing humility and devotion. Others bathe in the sacred ponds—Kumkum Kundam, Yoni Kundam, and Arihan Kundam—believed to purify the body and soul. The festival also features the Jogathi Nruthya, a ritual dance performed by the Jogathi community, who narrate Yellamma's story through song and movement.

The Joga Bedodu Ritual

The Joga Bedodu ritual, rooted in Renuka's penance, is still practiced by women in Karnataka and Telangana. Devotees bathe in a sacred lake or well, worship a Shivalinga, and beg for rice in nearby villages. The rice is divided, with half offered to priests or saints and the rest cooked with jaggery as a sacred offering. This ritual, performed over three days, is believed to cleanse sins and bring the goddess's blessings.

The Balkampet Yellamma Kalyanothsavam

In Hyderabad, the Balkampet Yellamma Temple hosts the Yellamma Kalyanothsavam during the Ashadha month. The temple, with its 10-foot-deep idol of the goddess, draws 200,000 to 600,000 devotees annually. Special rituals include offering naivedyam (food offerings) to the goddess, tying bead necklaces blessed by the priest, and bathing in the temple's sacred well. The Akhand Jyoti, a perpetually burning lamp, symbolizes the goddess's eternal presence.

Devadasi Initiation Ceremonies

Though rare today, the initiation of Joginis or Devadasis involves a sacred ceremony. The girl, accompanied by family and senior Joginis, visits the temple, where a priest offers naivedyam and blesses a bead necklace by touching it to the goddess's feet. The senior Jogini ties the necklace around the girl's neck, marking her dedication to Yellamma. The girl then takes vows to serve the goddess, fast on specific days, and beg with a metal mask of the deity. These vows emphasize service to the poor and non-retaliation, reflecting Yellamma's compassionate nature.

Symbols in Worship

Devotees often offer neem leaves, turmeric, and vermillion, which are sacred to Yellamma. The trident and lotus are placed near her altar, and in Telangana, her aniconic form is adorned with a sari. The Bonallu festival, celebrated before the rainy season, involves women carrying pots of food (bonam) on their heads to appease Yellamma and her sister goddesses, seeking protection from disease.

Part 5: Yellamma in the Modern World

As I walked through the bustling streets near the Balkampet Yellamma Temple in Hyderabad, I saw a blend of tradition and modernity. Devotees, young and old, thronged the temple, some in traditional attire, others in jeans and t-shirts, all united by their faith in Yellamma. Her worship has evolved, adapting to changing times while retaining its core essencc.

The Decline of the Devadasi System

The Devadasi system, once central to Yellamma's worship, has largely faded due to legal bans and social reforms. The British colonial government and later the Indian government passed laws in the 20th century to end the practice, citing exploitation. While this curbed the system's abuses, it also disrupted the lives of many Joginis, who lost their traditional roles without adequate support. Today, some Joginis continue to serve Yellamma through rituals and dance, but the practice is less visible, often conducted in secret to avoid legal scrutiny.

Controversies and Misconceptions

Yellamma's worship has faced criticism, particularly due to the Devadasi system's association with prostitution. Media reports and Western perspectives have sometimes sensationalized this, overlooking the spiritual and cultural significance of the practice. For devotees, the dedication of Joginis is a sacred act, not a commercial one. Efforts by activists and scholars, like Kancha Ilaiah, have sought to reframe Yellamma's worship as a subaltern tradition, rooted in the resilience of marginalized communities.

In 2015, an incident in Bengaluru highlighted the sensitivity around Yellamma's image. An Australian tourist was threatened for sporting a tattoo of the goddess on his shin, seen as disrespectful since it was below the knee. This incident sparked debates about cultural sensitivity and the deep reverence devotees have for Yellamma.

Tourism and Development

The Karnataka government has recognized the cultural and spiritual significance of the Yellamma Temple in Saundatti, approving the Sri Renuka Yellamma Kshetra Tourism Development Board in 2023 to develop it as a national tourist attraction. This initiative aims to preserve the temple's heritage, improve infrastructure, and promote its cultural identity. However, devotees hope this development will respect the sanctity of the site and avoid over-commercialization.

Yellamma in Popular Culture

Yellamma's story has inspired films like the Kannada "Sri Renukadevi Mahathme" (1977) and "Sri Renuka Devi" (2003), as well as the Marathi "Jai Renuka Devi Yellamma" (1985). These films portray her as a divine mother whose trials and triumphs inspire devotion. Her story also lives on in the oral traditions of the Jogathi community, who sing her praises through the Jogathi Nruthya.

She is a goddess born from fire, wronged by fate, yet resurrected as a symbol of hope and resilience. Her worship bridges the ancient and the modern, the elite and the marginalized, the spiritual and the cultural. In the bustling temples of Saundatti and Balkampet, in the quiet rituals of rural villages, and in the songs of the Jogathis, Yellamma lives on, a mother who embraces all who seek her.
Her story teaches us about forgiveness, strength, and the power of faith. Whether it's a devotee bathing in the sacred well to heal a skin ailment, a woman offering bonam to protect her family, or a Jogini dancing to her glory, Yellamma's presence is felt in every act of devotion. Her temples are not just stone structures but living spaces where communities come together, share their joys and sorrows, and find solace in her maternal embrace.
If you're ever in Saundatti during the Yellamma Jatre or in Hyderabad for the Kalyanothsavam, join the festivities—you'll feel the pulse of a tradition that has thrived for centuries.
Yellamma is more than a goddess; she is a mother, a protector, and a symbol of the enduring spirit of South India. Her legacy reminds us that divinity is not distant but woven into the lives of ordinary people, their struggles, and their faith. As her devotees say in Marathi, "Ude Gāṁ Āī

Ude"—"Rise, O Mother, rise." And rise she does, in every heart that calls her name.

Lord Murugan

When you hear the name Murugan, what comes to mind? A youthful warrior riding a majestic peacock, wielding a shining spear, radiating courage and wisdom? Or perhaps the vibrant festivals of Tamil Nadu, where devotees chant "Vetrivel Muruganukku Arogara" with fervor, carrying kavadis and piercing their bodies in devotion? For millions across South India, Sri Lanka, Malaysia, and beyond, Lord Murugan is more than a deity—he's a symbol of hope, strength, and spiritual awakening. His story is a tapestry woven with ancient myths, timeless beliefs, and heartfelt rituals that continue to inspire people today.

From his miraculous birth to his epic battles and tender love stories, Murugan's life teaches us about courage, love, and the pursuit of truth.

Let's start at the beginning—Murugan's extraordinary birth. According to Hindu mythology, Murugan wasn't born in the usual way. His arrival was a divine event, orchestrated to restore balance to the universe. The story begins with a demon named Tarakasura, who had grown so powerful that he threatened the gods themselves. Tarakasura had received a boon from Lord Brahma that made him nearly invincible—only a son of Lord Shiva could defeat him. The problem? Shiva, the great ascetic, was deep in meditation, uninterested in worldly affairs like marriage or children.

The gods, desperate for a savior, turned to Goddess Parvati, Shiva's divine consort. Parvati, an incarnation of Shakti (the cosmic feminine energy), performed intense penance to win Shiva's heart. Moved by her devotion, Shiva married her, and their union set the stage for Murugan's birth. But the story gets even more fascinating. According to the *Skanda Purana*, one of the major texts dedicated to Murugan, he wasn't born from Parvati's womb. Instead, Shiva released six divine sparks from his third eye, a symbol of his supreme wisdom and power. These sparks were so intense that Agni, the god of fire, was tasked with carrying them. Unable to bear their heat, Agni dropped them into the sacred river Ganga. The river, too, struggled with their energy and deposited them in a lotus-filled lake called Saravana Poigai. In this serene lake, the sparks transformed into six divine infants, each nurtured by one of the six Krittika stars (the Pleiades). These celestial mothers raised the babies with love, but when Parvati saw them, she embraced them so tightly that they merged into one being with six faces—Arumugam, the six-faced god. This is why Murugan is also called Kartikeya, meaning "son of the Krittikas." His six faces represent his ability to see in all directions, symbolizing infinite wisdom and awareness.

This extraordinary birth wasn't just a cosmic event—it was a promise of hope. Murugan was born to lead the divine army, defeat Tarakasura, and restore dharma (righteousness). His very existence is a reminder that even in the darkest times, a hero can emerge to set things right.

Murugan in Ancient Tamil Culture

While the *Skanda Purana* and other Sanskrit texts tell of Murugan's divine origins, his worship in South India, particularly among Tamils, has a unique flavor. Long before he was known as Shiva and Parvati's son, Murugan was revered as a tribal deity in ancient Tamil lands. In the Sangam literature (circa 300 BCE–300 CE), a collection of Tamil poems, he's called Ceyon, the "Red God" of the hills, or Kunrukkilavan, the "Lord of the Hills." The Tamils saw him as a youthful, radiant warrior who protected their lands and embodied the spirit of nature.

In texts like the *Tolkappiyam* (the oldest Tamil grammar text) and *Tirumurukarruppadai* (a devotional poem by Nakkirar), Murugan is celebrated as a god of valor, beauty, and justice. The ancient Tamils believed he resided in the hilly Kurinji region, a landscape of rugged beauty. They worshipped him with rituals led by a priest called the Velan, who would enter a trance-like state, adorned with red garlands and holding a spear (Vel), to channel Murugan's divine guidance. These rituals often involved offerings of rice, meat, and flowers, and were performed to seek blessings for love, health, or victory in battle.

What's fascinating is how Murugan's identity evolved over time. As Vedic culture from North India mingled with Dravidian traditions, Murugan was syncretized with Skanda, the warrior god of the north. Some scholars believe this blending began around 200 BCE, when North Indian dynasties like the Mauryas and later the Kadambas, Gangas, and Pallavas influenced South India. They saw similarities between Skanda, the commander of the gods' army, and Murugan, the Tamil war god with his iconic spear and peacock. Over time, the story of Murugan as Shiva's son became dominant, but his Tamil roots remained strong, especially in his association with the Vel and his role as a protector of the people.

Historical Evidence of Murugan's Worship

Murugan's worship isn't just a matter of stories—it's backed by archaeological evidence. Coins from the Yaudheya confederation in North India (circa 200 BCE–400 CE) feature images of Kartikeya, showing his prominence in early Hinduism. In South India, a Murugan temple from the Sangam period was unearthed at Saluvankuppam near Mamallapuram, revealed by the 2004 tsunami. This find, dated to the 8th century BCE or earlier, confirms that Murugan was a major deity in ancient Tamil culture.

By the time of the Chola dynasty (5th century BCE–13th century CE), Murugan's worship was firmly established. The Cholas, ardent devotees, built grand temples dedicated to him, like the one at Thiruparankundram. These temples became centers of devotion, art, and culture, showcasing Murugan's role as both a warrior and a teacher of Tamil literature and philosophy.

Murugan is more than a god of war—he's a multifaceted deity who embodies wisdom, courage, love, and spiritual growth. Let's explore the core beliefs that make him so beloved.

The God of War and Wisdom

At his core, Murugan is the commander of the divine army, a fierce warrior who battles evil forces. His Vel, a divine spear gifted by Parvati, symbolizes his power to destroy ignorance and negativity. But Murugan isn't just about physical strength. His six faces represent his ability to perceive all aspects of existence, making him a god of supreme intelligence. In the *Chandogya Upanishad,* he's called the "way that leads to wisdom," highlighting his role as a spiritual guide.

In Tamil tradition, Murugan is Thamizh Kadavul, the "God of the Tamils." He's seen as a teacher of poetry, literature, and dharma. The *Tiruppugazh,* a 15th-century anthology by Arunagirinathar, praises Murugan's wisdom and grace, describing him as a beacon of knowledge who inspires devotees to seek truth.

A Uniter of Traditions

One of Murugan's most beautiful qualities is his ability to bridge different Hindu traditions. He's revered in both Shaivism (which worships Shiva) and Vaishnavism (which worships Vishnu). As Shiva's son, he's central to Shaiva Siddhanta, a major Tamil spiritual tradition. Yet, his marriage to Devasena, the daughter of Indra (a Vedic god), ties him to Vaishnavism. This makes Murugan a symbol of unity, blending northern and southern, Vedic and Dravidian, warrior and philosopher.

The Eternal Youth

Murugan is often depicted as a youthful, vibrant god, riding his peacock with boundless energy. This eternal youth symbolizes staying young at heart, full of curiosity and passion. For devotees, Murugan inspires us to face life's challenges with enthusiasm and fearlessness, no matter our age.

Protector and Healer

Tamils believe Murugan protects against evil forces, both external (like enemies) and internal (like fear or doubt). His Vel is seen as a shield that dispels negative karma and diseases. Devotees chant mantras like "Om Saravana Bhava" or "Kanda Shashti Kavasam" to seek his protection and healing. These hymns, rooted in Tamil tradition, are believed to bring peace and strength.

Murugan's myths are like a treasure chest of stories—each one rich with lessons, emotions, and divine magic. Here are some of the most beloved tales that have been passed down through generations.

The Battle Against Surapadman

The most famous story of Murugan is his epic battle against the demon Surapadman. According to the *Skanda Purana* and Tamil texts like the *Kanda Puranam*, Surapadman was a demon king who received a boon that made him nearly invincible. He terrorized the heavens, imprisoning gods and saints. The gods pleaded for help, and Murugan, newly born, was appointed commander of the divine army.

Riding his peacock and wielding his Vel, Murugan led a fierce campaign. Surapadman, a master of illusion, transformed into a giant tree to evade him. But Murugan, with his divine insight, hurled his spear and split the tree in two. The two halves transformed into a peacock and a rooster. Instead of destroying them, Murugan showed compassion, making the peacock his vehicle and the rooster his banner. This act highlights his balance of strength and mercy, teaching us that true victory includes forgiveness.

This story is celebrated during the festival of Skanda Shashti, where devotees fast and pray to honor Murugan's triumph over evil. The battle symbolizes the inner struggle against ignorance and ego, with Murugan as the guide to spiritual victory.

The Contest for the Mango of Knowledge

Another beloved tale is the contest between Murugan and his brother, Ganesha, for the *jñāna-pazham* (fruit of wisdom). Sage Narada, known for stirring divine mischief, presented a magical mango to Shiva and Parvati, saying it should go to their wisest son. To decide, Shiva proposed a challenge: whoever circled the world three times first would win the fruit.

Murugan, confident in his speed, leapt onto his peacock and raced across the universe. Ganesha, however, took a different approach. Knowing his parents were the source of all creation, he circled Shiva and Parvati three times, saying, "You are my world." Impressed by Ganesha's wisdom, Shiva awarded him the mango. When Murugan returned and learned he'd lost, he felt disappointed and left Kailash to meditate in Palani, Tamil Nadu. There, he renounced worldly attachments, becoming a symbol of detachment and spiritual focus. The Palani Murugan Temple remains a major pilgrimage site, where devotees seek his blessings for wisdom and peace.

This story teaches us that wisdom isn't just about physical effort—it's about understanding what truly matters. Murugan's journey to Palani reminds us to let go of pride and seek inner clarity.

The Love Story of Murugan and Valli

Murugan's romantic side shines in his love story with Valli, a tribal girl. According to Tamil legend, Valli was found by a tribal chief, Nambi, in a forest pit dug for yams (hence her name, derived from "valli," meaning creeper). Raised as Nambi's daughter, Valli grew into a beautiful young woman who guarded her tribe's millet fields. Murugan, hearing of her beauty from Sage Narada, decided to win her heart.

Disguising himself as a hunter, Murugan approached Valli, but she was shy and reserved. Undeterred, he tried again as an old man, asking for food. When Valli's family interrupted, Murugan transformed into a tree to avoid detection. Later, he revealed his divine form, and Valli fell in love with him. Their romance faced challenges—Valli's family initially opposed the match due to their different backgrounds—but Murugan's persistence and divine charm won them over. Their marriage symbolizes love that transcends social barriers, uniting the divine with the human.

Murugan's marriage to Devasena, the daughter of Indra, is another key story. After defeating Surapadman, Indra offered Devasena to Murugan as a bride, representing the divine alliance between the gods and the celestial army. Together, Valli (earthly love) and Devasena (divine duty) reflect Murugan's ability to balance worldly and spiritual roles.

Murugan and Avvaiyar: The Lesson of Humility

One of my favorite stories involves Murugan and the Tamil poetess Avvaiyar. Once, Avvaiyar, a wise and respected poet, was resting under a tree, exhausted from her travels. A young boy—Murugan in disguise—approached and asked if she wanted "hot fruits" or "cool fruits." Confused, Avvaiyar chose cool fruits, thinking they'd be refreshing. The boy gave her some fruits and playfully asked if they were hot. When Avvaiyar blew on them to "cool" them, the boy laughed, saying, "Are they so hot you need to blow on them?"

Realizing the boy's divine nature, Avvaiyar bowed in reverence. Murugan revealed himself and taught her profound spiritual truths. Inspired, Avvaiyar composed devotional songs in his praise, which are still sung today. This story shows Murugan's playful yet profound nature, reminding us that wisdom often comes in humble forms.

Murugan as Swaminatha Swami: The Teacher of Shiva

In another remarkable tale, Murugan proves his wisdom surpasses even the gods. When Brahma, the creator, visited Mount Kailash, he disrespected young Murugan. Offended, Murugan asked Brahma to explain the meaning of the sacred mantra "Om." When Brahma failed, Murugan imprisoned him and took over creation. Alarmed, the gods sought Shiva's help. Shiva asked Murugan to explain the mantra, and Murugan delivered a profound discourse, teaching even his father. Impressed, Shiva called him Swaminatha Swami, the "Teacher of Shiva." This story, celebrated at the Swamimalai temple, highlights Murugan's supreme knowledge and his role as a guru.

The Significance of Murugan

Murugan's significance lies in his ability to inspire across multiple
dimensions. As a warrior, he teaches us to face challenges with courage. As a philosopher, he guides us toward wisdom. As a lover, he shows the power of devotion and connection. His six faces symbolize holistic awareness, his

Vel represents the destruction of ignorance, and his peacock signifies beauty and grace. In Tamil culture, he's a cultural icon, embodying the spirit of youth, valor, and creativity. Murugan also represents unity. His worship blends ancient Tamil traditions with Vedic Hinduism, making him a bridge between cultures. His festivals and temples are spaces where communities come together, celebrating shared faith and heritage. For devotees, Murugan is a friend, protector, and guide—a deity who feels close and relatable.

Rituals and Practices

Murugan's worship is vibrant and deeply personal, involving rituals that range from simple home prayers to elaborate temple ceremonies. Here are some key practices:

Daily Worship: Devotees offer flowers, fruits, milk, and sweets like *panchamritam* (a sacred mixture of banana, honey, ghee, jaggery, and cardamom) to Murugan's idol. Lighting camphor for *aarti* and chanting mantras like "Om Saravana Bhava" or "Vetrivel Muruganukku Arogara" are common.

Fasting and Vows: Many devotees observe fasts on days like Krittika Nakshatra (the star associated with Murugan) or during Skanda Shashti. These fasts are believed to purify the body and mind, drawing Murugan's blessings for health and success.

Kavadi Attam: This iconic ritual involves devotees carrying a *kavadi* (a decorated wooden structure) as an offering to Murugan, often during Thaipusam. Some pierce their bodies with small spears or hooks as a sign of penance, symbolizing their surrender to Murugan's will. The practice is linked to the story of Idumban, a devotee who carried two hills for Murugan and was granted a boon that devotees carrying kavadis would have their wishes fulfilled.

Chanting Sacred Texts: Hymns like the *Kanda Shashti Kavasam* and *Subrahmanya Bhujangam* (composed by Adi Shankaracharya) are recited for protection and spiritual growth. These texts are believed to have miraculous powers, with stories of devotees being healed or saved by chanting them.

Pilgrimages: The Arupadai Veedu (six abodes of Murugan) in Tamil Nadu—Thiruparankundram, Tiruchendur, Palani, Swamimalai, Thiruthani, and Pazhamudircholai—are major pilgrimage sites. Each temple is associated with a phase of Murugan's life, from his birth to his battles and marriages. Devotees visit these temples to seek blessings and complete spiritual journeys.

Major Festivals

Murugan's festivals are vibrant celebrations that bring communities together. Here are the most prominent ones:

Thaipusam: Held in the Tamil month of Thai (January–February), this festival commemorates Murugan receiving his Vel from Parvati to defeat Surapadman. Devotees undertake pilgrimages, carry kavadis, and perform *Kavadi Attam*, a dance of devotion. Thaipusam is especially grand at the Batu Caves in Malaysia and Palani in Tamil Nadu.

Skanda Shashti: Celebrated in Aippasi or Kartikai (October–November), this festival marks Murugan's victory over Surapadman. Devotees fast for six days, reciting the *Kanda Shashti Kavasam* and reenacting the battle through dramas and processions.

Panguni Uthiram: Held in Panguni (March–April), this festival celebrates Murugan's marriage to Devasena. Temples host grand processions, and devotees offer prayers for marital harmony.

Vaikasi Visakam: This marks Murugan's birthday in the month of Vaikasi (May–June). Temples are decorated, and devotees perform special pujas to honor his divine birth.

Karthika Deepam: A festival of lights in the month of Kartika (November–December), it's celebrated with lamps and prayers, especially in East India, where clay models of Murugan are worshipped by newlyweds.

Modern-Day Scene

Today, Murugan's worship is a global phenomenon, especially among Tamil communities. Temples like the Batu Caves in Malaysia, the Nallur Kandaswamy Temple in Sri Lanka, and the Murugan Temple in Sydney attract millions of devotees. The rise of technology has made his worship accessible—devotees can listen to *Kanda Shashti Kavasam* on apps, join virtual pujas, or share Murugan's stories on social media. Posts on X often highlight his festivals, with hashtags like #Thaipusam or #Murugan trending during

celebrations.
Murugan's influence extends beyond religion. In Tamil cinema and literature, he's a symbol of cultural pride. Songs and movies often reference his valor or his love for Valli. His temples are also hubs of charity, providing food, education, and healthcare to communities. In a fast-paced world, Murugan's eternal youth and wisdom remind us to stay grounded yet hopeful.

His birth from divine sparks shows us that even the impossible can become reality with purpose and faith. His battles teach us to confront our fears with courage. His love for Valli and Devasena reminds us that devotion can bridge any divide. And his wisdom, shared with poets like Avvaiyar and even his father Shiva, inspires us to seek knowledge with humility.

Murugan is a god for all seasons—a warrior when we need strength, a teacher when we seek truth, and a friend when we feel lost. His rituals, from carrying kavadis to chanting hymns, are ways to connect with his divine energy. His festivals, filled with music, dance, and devotion, bring communities together in joy and faith. Whether you're a Tamil devotee chanting "Muruga, Muruga" or someone new to his story, there's something universal in his message: face life with courage, love with an open heart, and seek wisdom above all.

So, the next time you visit a Murugan temple or hear his name, take a moment to feel his presence. He's not just a god; he's a guide, a protector, and a source of endless inspiration.

The Eternal Love Story of Kamadeva and Rati

Love is a force that moves hearts, sparks dreams, and binds souls. In Hindu mythology, no one embodies this force more beautifully than Kamadeva, the god of love, and his divine consort, Rati, the goddess of passion and desire. Their story is not just about romance—it's about devotion, sacrifice, and the power of love to overcome even the greatest obstacles. For centuries, their tales have inspired poets, artists, and devotees, reminding us that love is both a divine gift and a cosmic responsibility.

Kamadeva: The God of Love and Desire

Kamadeva, often called Kama, is the Hindu god of love, desire, and attraction. His name comes from the Sanskrit word *kama*, meaning "desire" or "longing." He is the divine force that stirs hearts, kindles passion, and ensures the continuation of life through love. In Hindu thought, desire is not just a human emotion—it's a cosmic principle that drives creation and sustains the universe. Kamadeva is the embodiment of this principle, a deity who wields the power to awaken love in gods, humans, and even demons.

The origins of Kamadeva are traced back to ancient Hindu scriptures, including the *Rig Veda* and *Atharva Veda*, some of the oldest sacred texts in the world. In the *Atharva Veda*, Kamadeva is described as a powerful god, "born at first, whom neither the gods nor the fathers ever equaled". This suggests that Kama is not just a deity but a primal force, older and greater than many other gods. In later texts like the *Puranas* and *Mahabharata*, Kamadeva is portrayed as a handsome young man, often compared to the Western Cupid, but with a deeper, more spiritual role.

Different scriptures offer varying accounts of Kamadeva's birth. In some, he is a *manasaputra* (mind-born son) of Brahma, the creator god, brought into existence to spread love and ensure the propagation of life. In the *Taittiriya Brahmana*, he is the son of Dharma (righteousness) and Shraddha (faith), symbolizing that love is rooted in virtue and devotion. Another version in the *Harivamsa* names Lakshmi, the goddess of prosperity, as his mother, linking love with abundance and beauty. Some stories even connect him to Lord Vishnu and Goddess Lakshmi, portraying him as their son, emphasizing his divine lineage.

Kamadeva is depicted as a youthful, charming deity with golden wings, riding a parrot or sometimes an elephant. His most iconic feature is his sugarcane bow, strung with a line of honeybees, and his flower-tipped arrows, each adorned with fragrant blossoms like jasmine, lotus, and mango flowers. These arrows don't just spark romantic love—they awaken desire in all its forms, from the longing for beauty to the drive for creation. His parrot, a symbol of communication, reflects how love speaks to the heart, while the fish on his red flag represents fertility and the flow of emotions.

Rati: The Goddess of Passion and Devotion

Rati, whose name comes from the Sanskrit root *ram* meaning "to delight" or "enjoy," is the goddess of love, passion, and sexual pleasure. She is Kamadeva's eternal companion, his muse, and his equal in the realm of desire. While Kamadeva ignites the spark of love, Rati nurtures its emotional and physical depth, embodying the joy and intimacy that love brings. Her name is synonymous with pleasure, but in Hindu thought, this pleasure is sacred, a path to spiritual connection when guided by devotion.

Rati's origin is as enchanting as her persona. The *Kalika Purana* tells a captivating story of her birth. After Brahma created Kamadeva to spread love, he realized Kama needed a partner. When Brahma and the Prajapatis (progenitor deities) became infatuated with Brahma's daughter Sandhya (Twilight), their impure desires caused them to tremble and sweat. From the sweat of Prajapati Daksha, a radiant woman emerged—Rati. Daksha presented her to Kamadeva as his wife, and their bond was instant, a union of divine love and passion. Another version in the *Brahma Vaivarta Purana* says Sandhya, after committing suicide due to Brahma's inappropriate affection, was resurrected by Vishnu as Rati and married to Kamadeva. Some texts even suggest Shiva as her father, adding another layer of divine connection.

Rati is described as breathtakingly beautiful, with jasmine-like skin, lotus-like eyes, and a radiant glow that captivates even the gods. She carries a discus and a lotus, symbols of protection and purity, and her arms are compared to lotus stalks, signifying grace and strength. In temple art, she is often shown alongside Kamadeva, her presence amplifying his charm. Her beauty is not just physical—it's a divine power that can enchant Kamadeva himself, making her a goddess who holds sway over the god of love.

The Divine Union

The love story of Kamadeva and Rati is one of the most profound in Hindu mythology. Their bond is not just romantic but cosmic, representing the balance of desire and devotion. In some stories, Rati was initially plain-looking and longed for beauty to win Kamadeva's heart. Goddess Lakshmi, moved by her devotion, taught her the art of *solah shringara* (sixteen adornments), transforming her into the most beautiful woman in the three worlds. Kamadeva, bewitched by her charm, made her his chief consort, and their love became a symbol of harmony and prosperity.

Their union is often compared to other divine couples like Krishna and Radha or Shiva and Parvati, symbolizing the eternal dance of love and attraction. In Vaishnavism, Kamadeva and Rati are sometimes seen as manifestations of Krishna and the Vraja girls, embodying divine love in its purest form. Their children, Harsha (Joy) and Yashas (Grace), reflect the fruits of their love—happiness and glory born from passion and devotion.

Historical Context in Hindu Scriptures

Kamadeva and Rati appear across a wide range of Hindu texts, from the ancient *Vedas* to the later *Puranas* and epics like the *Mahabharata* and *Ramayana*. In the *Rig Veda*, *kama* is a philosophical concept, a primal force of desire that drives creation. Over time, this concept personified into Kamadeva, the deity, and Rati, his consort, giving human form to abstract ideas. The *Puranas*—like the *Shiva Purana*, *Vishnu Purana*, and *Kalika Purana*—flesh out their stories, portraying them as active participants in divine dramas.

In the *Mahabharata*, Kamadeva is linked to Krishna's lineage, with his reincarnation as Pradyumna, Krishna's son, and Rati as Mayavati, highlighting their enduring presence in Hindu mythology. The *Ramayana* uses metaphors of Kamadeva's arrows to describe love's intensity, such as when Rama feels desire watching dancing peacocks. These texts show that Kamadeva and Rati are not just romantic figures but symbols of love's role in maintaining cosmic balance.

Their stories also appear in medieval texts like the *Kama Sutra* and *Ritikal* poetry (14th–17th centuries), which explore love and desire through the lens of Kamadeva and Rati. These works, named after them, reflect their cultural significance, portraying love as both a physical and spiritual experience. In temple art, such as at Khajuraho and the Madan Kamdev Temple in Assam, their images as "welcome sculptures" symbolize prosperity and the sanctity of love.

Beliefs Surrounding Kamadeva and Rati

In Hinduism, Kamadeva and Rati are revered as more than just gods of romance. They represent the sacred interplay of desire (*kama*) and pleasure (*rati*), essential for life's continuation and spiritual growth. Here are some core beliefs associated with them:

Love as a Cosmic Force

Hindu philosophy considers *kama* one of the four *purusharthas* (goals of life), alongside *dharma* (duty), *artha* (wealth), and *moksha* (liberation). Kamadeva, as the deity of *kama*, ensures that desire serves a higher purpose, guiding beings toward love and procreation while keeping it within the bounds of righteousness. Rati complements this by embodying the emotional and physical joy of love, making it a fulfilling experience.

Devotion and Sacrifice

Rati's unwavering devotion to Kamadeva, especially in the face of his destruction by Shiva, is a powerful symbol of love's resilience. Her penance and prayers to restore him reflect the belief that true love requires sacrifice and dedication. This makes her a figure of inspiration for devotees seeking strong, harmonious relationships.

Auspiciousness and Prosperity

Kamadeva and Rati are often depicted in temple carvings as symbols of good fortune. Their presence at marriage ceremonies, where the bride's feet are painted with Kamadeva's parrot, signifies blessings for love and fertility. Their association with Lakshmi links love with prosperity, reinforcing the idea that a loving relationship brings abundance.

Spiritual Love

In Vaishnavism, Kamadeva and Rati are seen as reflections of divine love, akin to Krishna and Radha. Their stories teach that love, when pure and devoted, can lead to spiritual liberation. This elevates their role beyond physical desire to a path toward union with the divine.

Balance of Masculine and Feminine

Kamadeva and Rati represent the balance of masculine and feminine energies. While Kamadeva sparks desire, Rati nurtures its emotional depth, creating a harmonious partnership. This balance is celebrated in rituals and art, where they are always depicted together, symbolizing unity.

The origins and beliefs surrounding Kamadeva and Rati paint a picture of love as a divine, multifaceted force. Kamadeva, with his sugarcane bow and flower arrows, awakens the spark of desire, while Rati, with her radiant beauty and devotion, deepens it into a lasting bond. Their stories, rooted in ancient scriptures, show that love is not just a fleeting emotion but a cosmic principle that drives creation and harmony. In Part 2, we'll dive into the captivating myths and legends that bring their love story to life, from Kamadeva's daring encounter with Shiva to Rati's heroic efforts to reunite with her beloved. These tales will reveal the depth of their bond and the sacrifices they made for love.

Myths and Legends of Kamadeva and Rati

Our journey begins with a story from the *Kalika Purana*, which tells how Kamadeva and Rati came to be together. Long ago, when Brahma, the creator god, sought to expand the universe, he created Kamadeva from his mind to spread love and desire. But Kamadeva needed a partner to fulfill his purpose. Brahma's daughter, Sandhya (Twilight), caught the eye of the Prajapatis, who were overcome with improper desire. Embarrassed by their feelings, they trembled and sweated, and from the sweat of Prajapati Daksha, a beautiful woman emerged—Rati. Brahma presented her to Kamadeva, and their connection was immediate, a spark that lit the cosmos with love.

In another version from the *Brahma Vaivarta Purana*, Sandhya, shamed by Brahma's affection, took her own life. Vishnu, moved by her plight, resurrected her as Rati and united her with Kamadeva. This tale highlights Rati's divine rebirth and her destined role as Kamadeva's beloved. In some accounts, Rati was plain-looking until Lakshmi blessed her with the art of *solah shringara*, making her the most beautiful woman in the three worlds. Kamadeva, enchanted by her charm, made her his chief consort, and their love became a symbol of divine harmony.

These stories show that Kamadeva and Rati's union was no accident—it was ordained by the gods to ensure that love would flourish in the world. Their bond, born from divine intervention, set the stage for their epic adventures.

Kamadeva's Sacrifice and Shiva's Wrath

The most famous legend of Kamadeva and Rati is the tale of Kamadeva's incineration by Lord Shiva, a story found in the *Shiva Purana* and other texts. It's a tale of courage, love, and rebirth that has resonated through the ages.

Long ago, the demon Tarakasura wreaked havoc on the heavens, terrorizing the gods. A prophecy revealed that only a son of Shiva could defeat him. But Shiva, grieving the loss of his wife Sati, had retreated into deep meditation on Mount Kailash, oblivious to the world and its needs. The gods, desperate to save the cosmos, turned to Kamadeva for help. They asked him to awaken Shiva's heart with love for Parvati, Sati's reincarnation, so they could marry and produce a son.

Kamadeva, accompanied by Rati and the spirit of spring (Vasanta), set out on this dangerous mission. He transformed himself into a sweet-scented breeze to slip past Shiva's guards and created a springtime atmosphere with blooming flowers and chirping birds. Finding the perfect moment, Kamadeva aimed his sugarcane bow and shot a flower-tipped arrow straight into Shiva's heart. The arrow worked—Shiva's eyes opened, and he saw Parvati, instantly captivated by her beauty. Love stirred in his heart, and the stage was set for their union.

But Shiva, realizing his meditation had been disturbed, grew furious. In a flash, he opened his third eye, and a blaze of fire consumed Kamadeva, reducing him to ashes. The world fell silent, for without Kamadeva, love vanished from the earth. Rati, witnessing her husband's destruction, was heartbroken. Overcome with grief, she smeared herself with his ashes and vowed to bring him back, even if it meant defying the gods themselves.

Rati's sorrow moved Parvati, who pleaded with Shiva to show mercy. Shiva, softened by Parvati's compassion, promised that Kamadeva would be reborn, but in a bodiless form as Ananga (the one without a body). He would live on as the spirit of love, filling every heart with desire. Shiva also foretold that Kamadeva would be reborn as Pradyumna, the son of Krishna and Rukmini, and reunite with Rati.

This legend is central to Kamadeva and Rati's mythology. It shows Kamadeva's sacrifice for the greater good and Rati's unwavering devotion, proving that love can endure even death. The story is also linked to the festival of Holi, where the bonfire symbolizes Kamadeva's burning, and offerings of sandalwood and mango blossoms honor his sacrifice.

The Rebirth of Kamadeva and Rati's Reunion

The story continues in the *Vishnu Purana* and *Harivamsa*, where Kamadeva's rebirth as Pradyumna and Rati's role as Mayavati unfold in a tale of adventure and love. After Kamadeva's incineration, Rati, guided by divine voices, performed severe penance to win back her husband. Shiva instructed her to seek work in the kitchen of the demon Shambara, who was destined to be killed by Kamadeva's reincarnation.

Rati took the form of Mayavati, a maid in Shambara's household, and waited patiently. Meanwhile, in Dwaraka, Krishna and Rukmini welcomed their son, Pradyumna, who was Kamadeva reborn. But Shambara, knowing Pradyumna was fated to destroy him, kidnapped the infant and threw him into the sea. A fish swallowed the baby, and when fishermen caught it, the fish ended up in Shambara's kitchen. Mayavati, recognizing the child as her beloved Kamadeva, rescued him and raised him in secret.

As Pradyumna grew, Mayavati taught him magic and combat skills to prepare him for his destiny. When he came of age, she revealed his true identity and their past as Kamadeva and Rati. Fueled by love and purpose, Pradyumna confronted Shambara, using the skills Mayavati taught him to defeat the demon in battle. With Shambara vanquished, Pradyumna and Mayavati (Rati) returned to Dwaraka, where they were reunited with Krishna and Rukmini. Their love, tested by separation and trials, emerged stronger than ever.

This story is a powerful reminder that true love transcends time, death, and even divine curses. Rati's determination and Pradyumna's bravery show that love is not just a feeling but a force that can conquer any obstacle.

Kamadeva's Mischief with Brahma

Another charming tale from the *Kalika Purana* shows Kamadeva's playful side. When Brahma created Sandhya, his daughter, the Prajapatis and even Brahma himself were overcome with desire for her. Kamadeva, eager to test his powers, shot his arrows at them, causing chaos. Shiva, witnessing this, laughed at their folly, and the embarrassed gods sweated profusely. From Daksha's sweat, Rati was born, and Brahma, to restore order, gave her to Kamadeva as his wife. But Brahma cursed Kamadeva for his mischief, foretelling that Shiva would one day burn him to ashes—a prophecy that later came true.

This story highlights Kamadeva's role as a cosmic trickster, using his arrows to stir emotions, even among the gods. It also sets the stage for his eventual sacrifice, showing that even divine playfulness has consequences.

Rati's Role in Other Myths

Rati is not just Kamadeva's consort—she's a powerful goddess in her own right. In one story from the *Puranas*, Indra, the king of the gods, called upon Rati to distract the sage Narada from his intense penance, which was threatening the cosmic order. Rati, with her enchanting beauty, succeeded in breaking Narada's focus, proving her ability to wield desire as a divine tool.

In Tantric traditions, Rati appears in the iconography of the Mahavidya goddess Chhinnamasta, who is depicted standing on Kamadeva and Rati in a sexual embrace. This image symbolizes the control of desire (when Chhinnamasta is dominant) or the celebration of sexual energy (when depicted non-suppressively), showing Rati's complex role as both a spiritual and sensual figure.

The myths of Kamadeva and Rati are rich with drama, devotion, and divine intervention. From Kamadeva's daring mission to awaken Shiva's heart to Rati's relentless quest to reunite with her beloved, their stories show that love is a force that can challenge gods, defeat demons, and transcend death. These tales, drawn from sacred texts, remind us that love requires courage, sacrifice, and faith. In Part 3, we'll explore the significance of Kamadeva and Rati in Hindu culture, their rituals, their presence in modern times, and how their legacy continues to inspire us today.

Significance of Kamadeva and Rati

Cosmic Balance and Creation

In Hindu thought, Kamadeva and Rati are essential to the cosmic order. Kamadeva's role as the god of desire ensures that life continues through love and procreation. Without desire, the cycle of creation would stall, and the universe would falter. Rati, as the goddess of passion, complements this by making love a joyful and fulfilling experience. Together, they maintain the balance between creation and enjoyment, ensuring that life is not just sustained but celebrated.

Their significance is rooted in the concept of *kama* as one of the four *purusharthas*. While *dharma* guides duty and *moksha* leads to liberation, *kama* fuels the human experience, making life vibrant and meaningful. Kamadeva and Rati remind us that desire, when channeled with love and respect, is a divine gift, not a distraction from spirituality.

Symbol of Devotion and Resilience

Rati's devotion to Kamadeva, especially in the face of his destruction, is a powerful symbol of love's strength. Her penance, her willingness to take on a new form as Mayavati, and her efforts to protect and reunite with Pradyumna show that true love requires sacrifice and perseverance. For devotees, Rati is an inspiration to remain steadfast in relationships, even through challenges.

Kamadeva's sacrifice for the greater good—risking Shiva's wrath to save the cosmos—highlights the idea that love is not selfish. It's a force that serves others, whether by uniting Shiva and Parvati or sparking love in human hearts. Their story teaches that love is both a personal joy and a universal responsibility.

Cultural and Artistic Influence

Kamadeva and Rati have left an indelible mark on Indian culture. Their stories inspired texts like the *Kama Sutra*, *Rati Rahasya*, and *Ananga Ranga*, which explore love and intimacy through their divine lens. In *Ritikal* poetry, their dialogues mirror the conversations of lovers, blending sensuality with spirituality. Temple carvings at Khajuraho and the Madan Kamdev Temple in Assam depict them as symbols of prosperity and fertility, welcoming devotees with their radiant presence.

In art, Kamadeva is shown with his sugarcane bow and parrot, while Rati's beauty is captured in vivid colors and intricate details. These images remind us of love's vibrancy and its ability to transcend the material world. Bollywood films and modern literature often draw on their imagery, portraying love as a divine, transformative force.

Spiritual Connection

In Vaishnavism, Kamadeva and Rati are linked to Krishna and Radha, whose love represents the soul's yearning for the divine. Their stories elevate human love to a spiritual plane, showing that passion, when guided by devotion, can lead to liberation. This makes them revered not just as romantic figures but as guides to a higher understanding of love.

Rituals Dedicated to Kamadeva and Rati

While Kamadeva and Rati are not as widely worshipped as major deities like Shiva or Vishnu, their presence is felt in specific rituals, especially those related to love, marriage, and fertility. Here are some key rituals associated with them:

Kamadeva-Rati Puja

The *Kamadeva-Rati Puja* is a ritual performed by couples seeking to strengthen their relationship or by individuals hoping to find a loving partner. This puja is believed to enhance compatibility, deepen emotional bonds, and bless devotees with charm and attractiveness. It involves offerings of flowers (especially lotuses), sweets, and sandalwood paste, which are said to soothe Kamadeva's burns from Shiva's fire.

A common mantra chanted during this puja is dedicated to both Kamadeva and Rati, invoking their blessings for love and harmony. Devotees may also recite specific verses from the *Vedas* or *Puranas* to honor their divine union. The puja is often performed by priests, but couples can also conduct it at home with guidance.

Holi: The Festival of Love

The festival of Holi, celebrated with colors and bonfires, is closely linked to Kamadeva. The bonfire lit on the eve of Holi (*Holika Dahan*) commemorates Kamadeva's incineration by Shiva. Devotees offer sandalwood paste and mango blossoms to honor his sacrifice, believing it brings blessings for love and renewal. The vibrant colors of Holi reflect the joy and passion that Kamadeva and Rati bring to the world. In some regions, Holi is called *Madana-Mahotsava* or *Kama-Mahotsava*, directly celebrating Kamadeva's role as the god of love. Couples pray to him and Rati for a joyful and harmonious relationship, while young people seek their blessings for romance.

Marriage Ceremonies

Kamadeva and Rati are invoked during Hindu marriage rituals to

bless the couple with love and fertility. The bride's feet are often painted with images of Kamadeva's parrot, symbolizing the presence of love in the union. Offerings of flowers and prayers to the couple ensure a harmonious and passionate marriage.

In some traditions, couples visit temples like the Madan Kamdev Temple in Assam or the Khajuraho temples in Madhya Pradesh to seek Kamadeva and Rati's blessings. These temples, adorned with carvings of the divine couple, are considered sacred sites for love and marital harmony.

Tantric Practices

In Tantric traditions, Rati is revered for her association with *Rati Bhava*, the emotional state of love and desire. Practitioners invoke her to deepen emotional intimacy and spiritual connection in relationships. The depiction of Chhinnamasta standing on Kamadeva and Rati symbolizes the balance between desire and self-control, a key principle in Tantra.

Offerings and Symbols

Devotees offer lotuses, jasmine flowers, and sweets to Kamadeva and Rati, as these symbolize purity, beauty, and the sweetness of love. Rati's swan or Kamadeva's parrot may be included in rituals to represent communication and grace. In some regions, couples perform *aarti* (lamp offerings) to the couple, seeking their blessings for a fulfilling partnership.

Modern-Day Relevance

In today's world, Kamadeva and Rati remain relevant as symbols of love's enduring power. While their worship is not as widespread as that of major deities, their influence is felt in art, literature, and popular culture. Here's how they continue to inspire:

Art and Literature

Modern artists and writers draw on Kamadeva and Rati's imagery to explore themes of love and desire. Bollywood films, TV shows, and novels often reference their stories, portraying love as a divine force that transforms lives. The

Kama Sutra and other texts named after them continue to influence discussions on love and intimacy, blending sensuality with spirituality.

Festivals and Celebrations

Holi remains a vibrant celebration of Kamadeva and Rati's legacy, with its colors and bonfires symbolizing love's renewal. Valentine's Day, though a Western import, has also been linked to their mythology in India, with some calling Kamadeva the "Indian Cupid". Young people invoke their blessings for romance, keeping their spirit alive in modern relationships.

Relationship Guidance

Couples facing challenges in their relationships often turn to Kamadeva-Rati Puja for blessings. Astrologers and priests recommend this ritual to enhance compatibility and rekindle passion. The belief that Kamadeva and Rati can bestow charm and harmony makes them popular among those seeking love or marital bliss.

Spiritual Inspiration

In a world where love is often commercialized, Kamadeva and Rati remind us of its sacred roots. Their stories encourage us to view love as a balance of passion and devotion, a force that can elevate the soul. Spiritual seekers, especially in VaVedanta and Tantra, find inspiration in their tales of devotion and balance.

Temples and Sacred Sites

Temples like the Madan Kamdev Temple in Assam and the Khajuraho temples continue to attract devotees seeking love and fertility. These sites, adorned with carvings of Kamadeva and Rati, serve as reminders of their enduring presence in Hindu culture.

Summing Up: The Timeless Love of Kamadeva and Rati

The story of Kamadeva and Rati is a celebration of love in all its forms—passionate, devoted, and divine. Kamadeva, with his flower-tipped arrows, ignites the spark of desire, while Rati, with her radiant beauty, deepens it into a lasting bond. Their myths teach us that love is not just a feeling but a force that requires courage, sacrifice, and faith. From Kamadeva's sacrifice to Rati's devotion, their tales show that love can overcome death, defeat demons, and unite souls across lifetimes.

In Hindu culture, they are more than gods—they are symbols of the cosmic dance of creation and joy. Their rituals, from Holi to marriage ceremonies, keep their spirit alive, while their presence in art and literature continues to inspire. In the modern world, Kamadeva and Rati remind us to cherish love's sacredness, to balance passion with devotion, and to see relationships as a path to spiritual growth.

Lord Kubera

When you think of wealth, what comes to mind? Gold, jewels, a grand mansion, or perhaps the freedom to live life on your terms? In Hindu mythology, wealth is not just about money—it's about abundance, prosperity, and the responsible stewardship of resources. At the heart of this concept stands Lord Kubera, the god of wealth, a figure who embodies the balance between material riches and spiritual wisdom. His story is one of transformation, devotion, and divine responsibility, woven into the rich tapestry of Hindu scriptures like the *Ramayana*, *Mahabharata*, and *Puranas*. Let's embark on a journey to uncover who Kubera is, where he came from, and the beliefs that make him such a revered deity in Hinduism and beyond.

Who Is Lord Kubera?

Kubera, also known as Kuvera, Kuberan, or Vaishravana, is the divine treasurer of the gods in Hindu mythology. He is the guardian of the world's riches, the king of the Yakshas (nature spirits), and the protector of the northern direction, one of the eight *Dikpalas* (guardians of directions). Unlike many other deities, Kubera's role is unique—he doesn't create wealth like Goddess Lakshmi, the goddess of fortune, but he manages and distributes it, ensuring it flows to those who deserve it through righteousness and devotion. His story is not just about gold and gems; it's about the deeper meaning of prosperity, the importance of humility, and the balance between material and spiritual wealth.

Kubera is often depicted as a stout, pot-bellied figure with a radiant complexion, resembling the hue of lotus leaves. He carries a money bag or a pot overflowing with treasures, sometimes holding a mace or a pomegranate, symbols of power and abundance. His appearance is distinctive—ancient texts describe him with three legs, eight teeth, and occasionally one eye, reflecting his unique, almost otherworldly persona. In some traditions, he rides a mongoose, which spits jewels when squeezed, or a man, emphasizing his dominion over wealth and treasures hidden in the earth. His celestial city, Alakapuri, located near Mount Kailash in the Himalayas, is a place of unimaginable splendor, with golden streets and palaces adorned with precious gems.

But Kubera wasn't always the god of wealth. His journey from a mortal-like figure to a divine deity is a tale of perseverance, penance, and divine grace, rooted in the ancient texts of Hinduism. Let's dive into his origins to understand how he became the guardian of riches.

The Origins of Kubera: From Mortal to Divine

Kubera's story begins in the ancient Vedic texts, where he is described as a chief of evil spirits, a far cry from the revered deity he later became. According to Hindu mythology, Kubera is the son of the sage Vishrava and his wife Ilavida (or Illavida in some texts). Vishrava was a respected scholar and the grandson of Brahma, the creator god, which places Kubera in a divine lineage. However, Vishrava's second wife, Kaikesi, a demon princess, gave birth to Ravana, Kumbhakarna, Vibhishana, and Surpanakha, making Kubera the elder half-brother of these famous characters from the *Ramayana*. This familial connection sets the stage for one of the most intriguing aspects of Kubera's mythology—his rivalry with Ravana.

In the early Vedic texts, like the *Satapatha Brahmana*, Kubera is portrayed as a lord of thieves and criminals, associated with the darker aspects of wealth, such as greed and hoarding. Over time, however, his character evolved. The *Puranas* and epics like the *Ramayana* and *Mahabharata* elevate him to the status of a *Deva* (god), granting him the title of the god of wealth and the king of the Yakshas. This transformation is attributed to his intense devotion and penance, particularly towards Lord Shiva and Brahma.

One legend tells of Kubera's extraordinary tapasya (penance) to gain divine favor. According to the *Shiva Purana*, Kubera, originally named Gunnidhi, was a poor man consumed by greed. In a moment of desperation, he tried to steal from a Shiva temple but was moved by the divine light of a lamp he accidentally lit. Touched by his unintentional act of devotion, Lord Shiva appeared before him and granted him the boon of immortality and the role of the god of wealth. Another version in the *Ramayana* describes Kubera performing severe penance for thousands of years, standing on one leg or meditating underwater, to please Brahma. Impressed by his dedication, Brahma bestowed upon him the lordship of wealth, the guardianship of the northern direction, the Pushpaka Vimana (a flying chariot), and the city of Lanka.

These stories highlight a recurring theme in Hindu mythology: the power of devotion and discipline to transform one's destiny. Kubera's rise from a flawed, mortal-like figure to a divine treasurer underscores the idea that wealth, when earned through righteousness, is a divine gift.

Kubera's Family and the Lanka Connection

Kubera's family ties add depth to his story, connecting him to some of the most iconic figures in Hindu mythology. As the son of Vishrava and Ilavida, Kubera was born into a lineage of wisdom and divinity. His father's second marriage to Kaikesi introduced a complex dynamic, as Kubera's half-siblings—Ravana, Kumbhakarna, Vibhishana, and Surpanakha—belonged to the Rakshasa (demon) race. This familial divide sets the stage for one of the most famous legends about Kubera: his loss of Lanka to Ravana.

According to the *Ramayana*, Kubera was the original ruler of Lanka, a golden city built by the divine architect Vishvakarma. Lanka was a marvel of opulence, with palaces made of gold and gardens filled with divine flowers. However, Ravana, driven by ambition and greed, sought to claim Lanka for himself. Empowered by a boon from Brahma, Ravana challenged Kubera and overthrew him, seizing both the city and the Pushpaka Vimana. Distraught but resilient, Kubera left Lanka and established a new abode, Alakapuri, in the Himalayas near Lord Shiva's residence on Mount Kailash. This celestial city became a symbol of Kubera's divine renewal, a place where wealth and spirituality coexist in harmony.

Kubera's relationship with his half-siblings is a study in contrasts. While Ravana represents unchecked ambition and greed, Vibhishana, another half-brother, embodies righteousness and devotion, aligning himself with Lord Rama in the *Ramayana*. Kubera's own character lies somewhere in between—he is neither wholly demonic nor entirely divine, reflecting the complex nature of wealth itself. His marriage to Bhadra (also known as Kamini or Nalayani) and their children, including Nalakubara, further tie him to the divine realm, emphasizing the balance of material wealth and familial harmony.

Beliefs Surrounding Kubera

Kubera's role in Hindu mythology goes beyond being a mere dispenser of wealth. He embodies several key beliefs that resonate with devotees:

Wealth as a Divine Responsibility: Kubera is not just the god of wealth; he is its guardian and distributor. Unlike Lakshmi, who represents the creation of wealth and fortune, Kubera ensures its proper management and protection. Devotees believe that worshipping Kubera brings not only prosperity but also the wisdom to use wealth ethically.

Balance Between Material and Spiritual Wealth: Kubera's association with Lord Shiva, a deity of asceticism, underscores the importance of balancing material riches with spiritual growth. His stories teach that wealth, when misused, can lead to downfall, as seen in Ravana's fate, but when managed with humility, it can elevate one's life.

Guardianship of the North: As the *Dikpala* of the northern direction, Kubera is believed to protect the treasures hidden in the earth, such as minerals and jewels. His role as a *Lokapala* (world protector) extends to safeguarding cosmic order, ensuring that wealth flows in harmony with dharma (righteousness).

King of Yakshas: The Yakshas, semi-divine beings associated with nature and hidden treasures, are under Kubera's command. Devotees see him as a bridge between the human and divine realms, capable of granting access to the earth's secret riches through devotion and good deeds.

Connection to Other Deities: Kubera is often worshipped alongside Lakshmi during festivals like Diwali, symbolizing the synergy between fortune and wealth management. His devotion to Shiva and his role as a treasurer complement the functions of other deities like Vishnu and Ganesha, emphasizing the interconnectedness of divine forces.

These beliefs make Kubera a multifaceted deity, revered not only for material prosperity but also for the ethical and spiritual lessons his mythology imparts. His stories, filled with drama and moral teachings, bring these beliefs to life, making him a relatable figure for devotees seeking guidance in their pursuit of abundance.

Kubera's mythology is rich with tales that illustrate his divine authority, his interactions with gods and humans, and the lessons embedded in his journey. These stories, drawn from the *Ramayana*, *Mahabharata*, *Puranas*, and other texts, paint a vivid picture of a deity who is both powerful and complex. Let's explore some of the most famous legends about Kubera, each offering insights into his character and the values he represents.

The Tale of Kubera and Ravana: The Fall of Lanka

One of the most well-known stories about Kubera is his rivalry with his half-brother Ravana, the demon king of Lanka. As mentioned earlier, Kubera was the original ruler of Lanka, a city of unparalleled beauty and wealth. The *Ramayana* narrates how Ravana, driven by his insatiable desire for power, challenged Kubera's authority. Empowered by a boon from Brahma that made him nearly invincible, Ravana stormed Lanka, defeated Kubera's Nairrata army, and seized the city along with the Pushpaka Vimana, a magical flying chariot.

Kubera, though distressed, did not let this loss define him. With the blessings of Brahma and Shiva, he established Alakapuri, a new celestial city in the Himalayas. Alakapuri is described in the *Puranas* as a place of divine splendor, with golden streets, jewel-encrusted palaces, and gardens filled with celestial flowers. The city is inhabited by Yakshas, Kinnaras, and other mythical beings, all under Kubera's rule. This story highlights Kubera's resilience and ability to transform loss into renewal, a lesson for devotees facing setbacks in their pursuit of prosperity.

The tale also underscores the moral contrast between Kubera and Ravana. While Ravana's greed led to his eventual downfall in the *Ramayana*, Kubera's humility and devotion earned him divine favor. Devotees often reflect on this story as a reminder that true wealth is not about possession but about righteous stewardship.

Kubera and Ganesha: A Lesson in Humility

Another delightful story involves Kubera and Lord Ganesha, illustrating the dangers of pride and the importance of humility. According to the *Shiva Purana*, Kubera, proud of his immense wealth, once invited Lord Shiva and Goddess Parvati to a grand feast at Alakapuri to showcase his opulence. Shiva and Parvati, aware of Kubera's arrogance,

declined the invitation but sent their son Ganesha in their place.
Ganesha, known for his insatiable appetite, arrived at the feast and began devouring everything in sight—food, dishes, and even the furniture! Kubera, alarmed, realized his supplies were running out. In a panic, he rushed to Shiva for help. Shiva, with a knowing smile, gave Kubera a bowl of rice prepared by Parvati and instructed him to offer it to Ganesha with humility. When Kubera presented the rice with genuine respect, Ganesha's hunger was miraculously satisfied.

This story is a favorite among devotees, as it teaches that wealth alone cannot bring fulfillment. Kubera's pride in his riches was humbled by Ganesha's divine appetite, reminding us that true prosperity comes from devotion, humility, and gratitude. It also highlights Kubera's close relationship with Shiva, reinforcing his role as a deity who operates under divine guidance.

Kubera's Curse and the Gardener Hemamali

The *Padma Purana* tells a darker tale about Kubera's less forgiving side, revealing the complexities of his character. Kubera maintained a magnificent garden in Alakapuri, filled with divine flowers used for temple worship. He employed a gardener named Hemamali to tend to it daily. One day, Hemamali, distracted by a visit to Manasasaras (a sacred lake), neglected his duties and failed to deliver the flowers for Kubera's worship.

Furious at this lapse, Kubera summoned Hemamali and, in a fit of anger, cursed him to become a leper and banished him from Alakapuri. The story portrays Kubera as a strict ruler who values discipline and duty, reflecting his role as a guardian who ensures wealth is respected and managed responsibly. However, it also shows his capacity for mercy, as some versions suggest that Hemamali was later forgiven after seeking divine intervention.

This tale serves as a cautionary lesson about the consequences of negligence and the importance of fulfilling one's responsibilities, especially when entrusted with divine duties. It also humanizes Kubera, showing that even a god can have moments of anger, making him relatable to devotees.

Kubera and Lord Venkateswara: The Eternal Loan

A popular story in South India, particularly associated with the Tirupati Balaji temple, involves Kubera's financial dealings with Lord Venkateswara (an avatar of Vishnu). According to legend, Venkateswara needed funds to marry Goddess Padmavati. Kubera, as the divine treasurer, lent him a significant sum of money. To this day, devotees visiting the Tirupati temple offer donations to the *hundi* (donation pot) to help Venkateswara repay his debt to Kubera.

This story underscores Kubera's role as the keeper of divine wealth, trusted even by gods like Vishnu. It also reflects the belief that devotees can participate in cosmic narratives by contributing to sacred causes, reinforcing the idea that wealth is a shared
responsibility.

Kubera's Penance and Divine Elevation

The story of Kubera's penance is central to his mythology, as it marks his transformation from a mortal-like figure to a god. In one version from the *Puranas*, Kubera, born as Gunnidhi, was a greedy man who attempted to steal from a Shiva temple. Moved by an accidental act of devotion (lighting a lamp), Shiva granted him the boon of wealth and immortality. In another account, Kubera performed intense tapasya for thousands of years, meditating in extreme conditions to please Brahma or Shiva. His dedication earned him the titles of *Dhanapati* (Lord of Wealth), *Lokapala* (world protector), and *Dikpala* (guardian of the north), along with the Pushpaka Vimana and the city of Lanka.

These stories emphasize the transformative power of devotion and discipline, a recurring theme in Hindu mythology. Kubera's journey inspires devotees to pursue their goals with sincerity, reminding them that divine blessings come to those who align their actions with dharma.

Kubera's mythology is not just a collection of ancient stories; it holds profound significance in Hindu culture and continues to influence modern spiritual practices. His role as the god of wealth makes him a focal point for those seeking financial stability, but his teachings extend far beyond material riches. Let's explore the deeper meaning of Kubera's worship, the rituals associated with him, his relevance in today's world, and a reflection on his enduring legacy.

The Significance of Kubera in Hindu Mythology

Kubera's importance lies in his multifaceted role as a deity who bridges the material and spiritual realms. Here are some key aspects of his significance:

Stewardship of Wealth: Kubera is not just about accumulating wealth but managing it wisely. His role as the treasurer of the gods emphasizes the importance of using resources ethically and ensuring they benefit others. This resonates with devotees who seek not just prosperity but the wisdom to use it for good.

Symbol of Balance: Kubera's association with Shiva, a deity of detachment, highlights the need to balance material wealth with spiritual growth. His stories warn against greed (as seen with Ravana) and pride (as in the Ganesha tale), teaching that true prosperity includes humility and generosity.

Guardian of the North: As the *Dikpala* of the north, Kubera protects the treasures hidden in the earth, symbolizing the idea that wealth is a divine gift meant to be respected. His role as a *Lokapala* underscores his responsibility to maintain cosmic order, ensuring wealth flows in harmony with dharma.

King of Yakshas: The Yakshas, under Kubera's rule, are guardians of nature's treasures. This connection reflects the belief that wealth is tied to the natural world, and devotees must honor both the earth and its resources.

Interfaith Relevance: Kubera's presence extends beyond Hinduism to Buddhism (as Vaishravana or Jambhala) and Jainism (as Sarvanubhuti). His universal appeal as a deity of prosperity makes him a unifying figure across Indian religious traditions.

Rituals and Worship of Kubera

Worshipping Kubera is a way for devotees to seek financial stability, protection of wealth, and the wisdom to manage resources. His rituals are often performed alongside those of Goddess Lakshmi, as the two deities complement each other—Lakshmi brings fortune, while Kubera ensures its proper use. Here are some key rituals and practices associated with Kubera:

Kubera Puja: This sacred ritual is performed to invoke Kubera's blessings for prosperity. Devotees set up an altar facing the north (Kubera's direction), adorned with a Kubera Yantra (a mystical geometric diagram believed to attract wealth). Offerings include coins, gold, jewels, flowers, and sweets, symbolizing gratitude for abundance. The puja involves lighting diyas (oil lamps) and incense, chanting mantras, and offering prayers to Kubera and Lakshmi.

Kubera Mantras: Chanting specific mantras is a powerful way to connect with Kubera. Popular mantras include:

Om Yakshaya Kuberaya Vaishravanaya Dhanadhanyadi Pate Dhana Dhanya Samruddhim Me Dehi Dapaya Swaha: This mantra invokes Kubera's blessings for wealth and prosperity.

***Om Sham Kuberaya Namaha*:** A simpler mantra, chanted 108 times, to seek Kubera's favor. Devotees believe that regular chanting purifies the mind and attracts financial success.

Kubera Yantra: The Kubera Yantra is a sacred tool placed in homes, offices, or cash boxes to invite prosperity. It is typically installed in the northern part of a building, as this direction is associated with Kubera. The yantra is worshipped with offerings of sandalwood paste, flowers, and rice, believed to amplify its energy.

Festivals Dedicated to Kubera:

Dhanteras: The first day of the Diwali festival is dedicated to Kubera and Lakshmi. Devotees buy gold, silver, or utensils, believing that such purchases on this auspicious day bring lasting prosperity. Kubera Puja is performed in homes and businesses, with prayers for financial stability.

Akshaya Tritiya: Known as the "day of eternal wealth," this occasion is ideal for starting new ventures and seeking Kubera's blessings. Devotees perform pujas and invest in gold to honor Kubera's role as the treasurer of wealth.

Sharad Purnima: This full-moon day is considered Kubera's birthday, making it an auspicious time for his worship.

Offerings and Symbols: Offerings to Kubera often include lotus leaves, sesame seeds, and meat (in some ancient texts like the *Grihyasutras*). His symbols, such as the mongoose, money bag, and Pushpaka Vimana, are included in rituals to represent his dominion over wealth.

Temples Dedicated to Kubera

While Kubera is not worshipped with as many standalone temples as other deities, several sacred sites honor him:

Kubera Bhandari Temple in Gujarat, located on the banks of the Narmada River, is believed to be where Kubera performed penance to please Shiva.

Dhopeshwar Mahadev Temple in Madhya Pradesh, which features a unique idol of Shiva and Kubera together, symbolizing their divine connection. These temples are pilgrimage sites where devotees seek Kubera's blessings for prosperity.

Modern-Day Practices and Relevance

In today's fast-paced world, Kubera's relevance remains strong, especially for those navigating financial challenges or seeking success in business. His worship is particularly popular among merchants, traders, and entrepreneurs who view him as a patron of financial stability. Here's how Kubera's legacy thrives in modern times:

Business and Finance: Many business owners keep a Kubera Yantra in their offices or shops, believing it attracts customers and protects profits. Chanting Kubera mantras before starting a new venture is a common practice to ensure success.

Diwali Celebrations: Dhanteras, the first day of Diwali, is a major occasion for Kubera worship. Families clean their homes, light diyas, and perform Kubera-Lakshmi Puja to invite prosperity for the coming year. The tradition of buying gold or silver on Dhanteras reflects Kubera's association with precious metals.

Cultural Depictions: Kubera appears in modern Indian literature, films, and television, often as a symbol of wealth and abundance. His stories are used to teach lessons about financial responsibility and ethical wealth management.

Global Influence: Kubera's presence in Buddhism (as Vaishravana) and Jainism (as Sarvanubhuti) makes him a figure of universal appeal. In Buddhist monasteries and Jain temples, his iconography inspires devotees to seek both material and spiritual abundance.

Spiritual Lessons: Kubera's mythology resonates with modern audiences seeking balance in a materialistic world. His stories encourage ethical earning, generosity, and gratitude, reminding us that wealth is a tool for good when used wisely.

Summing Up: Kubera's Enduring Legacy

Lord Kubera's journey from a mortal-like figure to the god of wealth is a testament to the power of devotion, discipline, and righteousness. His stories, filled with drama, moral lessons, and divine interventions, offer a window into the values of Hindu mythology. Whether it's his rivalry with Ravana, his humbling encounter with Ganesha, or his eternal loan to Venkateswara, Kubera's tales remind us that wealth is more than money—it's about responsibility, humility, and spiritual growth.

In a world obsessed with material success, Kubera's teachings are a beacon of balance. His rituals, from chanting mantras to worshipping the Kubera Yantra, provide practical ways for devotees to connect with his energy. His presence in festivals like Dhanteras and Akshaya Tritiya keeps his legacy alive, while his universal appeal across Hinduism, Buddhism, and Jainism underscores his timeless relevance.

As we reflect on Kubera's story, we're reminded that true prosperity comes from aligning our actions with dharma, respecting the divine gifts we receive, and sharing our abundance with others. So, the next time you light a diya on Dhanteras or chant a Kubera mantra, remember that you're not just seeking wealth—you're invoking the wisdom to use it for a higher purpose.

Bhairav Baba and the Kaal Bhairav Temple

When you step into the ancient city of Varanasi, with its winding lanes and the sacred Ganga flowing gently by, you can feel a divine energy in the air. Among the countless temples that dot this spiritual capital of India, one stands out for its fierce yet protective aura—the Kaal Bhairav Temple. Dedicated to Bhairav Baba, also known as Kaal Bhairav, this temple is not just a place of worship but a symbol of time, justice, and divine protection.

Who Is Bhairav Baba?

Bhairav Baba, or Lord Kaal Bhairav, is one of the most fascinating and fearsome deities in Hinduism. To understand him, we must first know his roots. Bhairav is a fierce manifestation of Lord Shiva, the destroyer in the Hindu trinity of Brahma, Vishnu, and Shiva. The name "Bhairav" comes from the Sanskrit word *bhīru*, meaning "fearsome" or "terrifying." Yet, despite his intimidating appearance, Bhairav Baba is a protector, a guardian, and a remover of obstacles for those who approach him with devotion. He is often depicted as a dark, fierce figure with bulging eyes, a garland of skulls around his neck, and a trident or rod in his hand. His loyal companion, a black dog, is always by his side, symbolizing vigilance and loyalty.

In Hindu mythology, Bhairav is not just one deity but a collective of forms, with Kaal Bhairav being the most prominent. The term *Kaal* means "time" or "death," signifying his role as the master of time, the one who governs the cycle of life and death. Devotees believe that Kaal Bhairav controls the flow of time, ensuring that everything happens according to the cosmic order. He is both a destroyer of evil and a protector of the righteous, a deity who punishes wrongdoers but showers blessings on those who seek his guidance.

Bhairav Baba is revered across India, Nepal, and beyond, especially in Shaivism (the sect of Hinduism that worships Shiva) and Tantric traditions. In Varanasi, he is lovingly called the *Kotwal of Kashi*, meaning the "guardian" or "police chief" of the holy city. It is said that no one can enter or leave Kashi without his permission, and even Yama, the god of death, must seek Kaal Bhairav's approval before touching anyone in this sacred land. This belief makes the Kaal Bhairav Temple a must-visit for pilgrims, as a trip to Varanasi is considered incomplete without paying homage to Bhairav Baba.

The Origins of Kaal Bhairav: A Divine Tale

The story of Kaal Bhairav's origin is steeped in Hindu mythology, particularly in the Puranas, which are ancient Hindu texts that narrate the stories of gods and goddesses. One of the most popular legends comes from the *Shiva Mahapurana* and is widely accepted among devotees. Let me share this tale as I heard it from the priests and locals of Varanasi, a story that captures the power and purpose of Kaal Bhairav.

Long ago, in the cosmic realm, a heated argument broke out among the three supreme gods of the Hindu trinity—Brahma (the creator), Vishnu (the preserver), and Shiva (the destroyer). The dispute was about who among them was the most powerful and supreme. Brahma, known for his role in creating the universe, grew arrogant and claimed superiority, boasting that his five heads made him equal to Shiva. Vishnu, calm and wise, tried to mediate, but Brahma's pride only grew. He began interfering in Shiva's divine duties, mocking him and asserting his dominance.

Shiva, known for his calm demeanor but fiery temper when provoked, could not tolerate Brahma's arrogance. In a moment of divine rage, Shiva plucked a tiny nail from his finger and threw it to the ground. From that nail emerged Kaal Bhairav, a terrifying figure with a dark complexion, fiery eyes, and a fierce presence. Riding a black dog and wielding a trident, Kaal Bhairav charged toward Brahma. With one swift motion, he severed one of Brahma's five heads, teaching the creator a lesson in humility. The severed head, known as *Brahma Kapala* (Brahma's skull), stuck to Kaal Bhairav's hand as a symbol of his act.

However, cutting off Brahma's head was no small matter. Brahma was a revered deity, and killing a Brahmin (even a divine one) was considered a grave sin, known as *Brahmahatya*. To atone for this sin, Shiva instructed Kaal

Bhairav to wander the earth as a naked ascetic, carrying Brahma's skull as a begging bowl. Kaal Bhairav roamed the world, visiting holy places and seeking liberation from the curse. No matter where he went, the sin followed him like a shadow. Finally, he reached the sacred city of Kashi (Varanasi). The moment he stepped into this holy land, the Brahma Kapala fell from his hand, and the sin of Brahmahatya vanished into the netherworld. Kashi became the place where Kaal Bhairav was purified, and Shiva declared him the eternal guardian of the city.

This story, found in texts like the *Skanda Purana* and *Shiva Mahapurana*, is central to the identity of Kaal Bhairav. It portrays him as a deity born from Shiva's wrath to restore cosmic balance, punish ego, and uphold dharma (righteousness). Devotees see this tale as a reminder that pride and arrogance lead to downfall, and only humility and devotion can bring redemption.

Other Origin Stories

While the Brahmahatya story is the most well-known, other legends offer different perspectives on Kaal Bhairav's origin, each adding depth to his divine persona. Another tale from the *Puranas* speaks of Kaal Bhairav's creation to defeat a demon named Dahurasuran. This demon had received a boon that he could only be killed by a woman. Goddess Parvati, Shiva's consort, took the form of Kali to slay the demon. After the battle, Kali's wrath gave birth to a child, who merged with Shiva to become Kaal Bhairav. From him emerged the eight forms of Bhairav, known as the *Ashta Bhairavas*, each guarding a specific direction and aspect of life.

In another story, Kaal Bhairav is linked to the tale of Sati and Daksha. Sati, Shiva's first wife and daughter of King Daksha, married Shiva against her father's wishes. Daksha, a staunch Vaishnavite, despised Shiva for his unconventional ways and refused to invite him to a grand yagna (sacrificial ritual). Sati attended the yagna alone but was insulted by her father. Unable to bear the dishonor to her husband, she immolated herself in the sacrificial fire. Enraged, Shiva created Kaal Bhairav (and another deity, Veerabhadra) to destroy Daksha's yagna and behead him. This story highlights Kaal Bhairav's role as a protector of Shiva's honor and a destroyer of evil forces.
In Tantric traditions, Bhairav is seen as a manifestation of Shiva's
supreme consciousness, representing the ultimate reality (*Para Brahman*). In Kashmir Shaivism, as taught by the 11th-century philosopher Abhinavagupta, Bhairav is not just a deity but a state of divine awareness, embodying both creation and destruction. This philosophical perspective adds a deeper layer to Bhairav's identity, making him a symbol of transcendence for spiritual seekers.

A Historical Perspective

The Kaal Bhairav Temple in Varanasi, located near the Vishwanath Gali, is one of the oldest and most revered temples dedicated to Bhairav Baba. Varanasi, also known as Kashi, is one of the holiest cities in Hinduism, believed to be the abode of Lord Shiva. The temple's history is intertwined with the city's spiritual legacy, which spans thousands of years. While exact historical records about the temple's construction are scarce, it is believed to date back to ancient times, possibly as early as the Vedic period, with renovations and expansions by later rulers, including the Marathas in the 18th century.

The temple's architecture reflects traditional North Indian Hindu styles, with intricate stone carvings depicting scenes from Hindu mythology. The main shrine houses a silver-faced idol of Kaal Bhairav, adorned with a garland of skulls and peacock feathers. His vahana, the black dog, is depicted beside him, symbolizing loyalty and vigilance. The idol is often covered with a cloth, except during special festivals like Bhairava Ashtami, when it is fully revealed, adorned with silver skulls and other offerings.

Historically, the Kaal Bhairav Temple has been a center of pilgrimage and devotion. It is said that the temple was established at the very spot where Kaal Bhairav was absolved of the Brahmahatya sin. Over the centuries, it has been maintained by religious trusts and local authorities, preserving its spiritual and cultural significance. The temple's location in Varanasi, near the Kashi Vishwanath Temple (dedicated to Shiva), underscores its importance, as devotees believe that visiting Kaal Bhairav completes their pilgrimage to Kashi.

Beliefs Surrounding Kaal Bhairav

The beliefs surrounding Bhairav Baba are as diverse as his forms, yet they all center on his role as a protector and enforcer of justice. Here are some of the most common beliefs held by devotees:

Guardian of Kashi: Kaal Bhairav is revered as the *Kotwal* or guardian of Varanasi. Devotees believe he protects the city and its inhabitants from evil forces, black magic, and negative energies. It is said that even death cannot enter Kashi without his permission, making the city a place of liberation (*moksha*).

Master of Time: As the deity of time, Kaal Bhairav teaches devotees to respect time and use it wisely. He is believed to help with time management, discipline, and overcoming procrastination. Devotees pray to him for success in endeavors that require focus and timeliness.

Remover of Obstacles: Like Lord Ganesha, Kaal Bhairav is seen as a remover of obstacles, especially those caused by enemies, negativity, or spiritual afflictions. People visit his temple to seek protection from black magic, evil spirits, and tantric influences.

Punisher of Sins: Kaal Bhairav is known as *Dandapani*, meaning "one who holds a rod to punish sinners." Devotees believe he maintains law and order in the cosmic realm, punishing those who stray from dharma and rewarding the righteous.

Healer of Ailments: Many devotees believe that worshipping Kaal Bhairav can cure physical and mental ailments, including serious illnesses and psychological disorders. Offerings like liquor, believed to be consumed by the deity, are distributed as prasad and considered to have healing powers.

Protector of Travelers: Kaal Bhairav is the guardian of travelers, especially those journeying at night or over long distances. Before embarking on a trip, devotees offer prayers and light mustard oil lamps to seek his protection.

Spiritual Growth: Worshipping Kaal Bhairav is believed to foster spiritual development by helping devotees overcome fears, especially the fear of death. He is seen as a guide to liberation, leading devotees toward self-realization and moksha.

These beliefs make Kaal Bhairav a deity who is both feared and loved. His fierce form may intimidate, but his compassionate nature draws devotees seeking solace, strength, and spiritual growth.

The Many Forms of Bhairav

Kaal Bhairav is not a singular deity but part of a larger group of Bhairav manifestations. According to Hindu texts, there are 52 forms of Bhairav, grouped under eight primary forms known as the *Ashta Bhairavas*. Each form has a unique role and grants specific boons to devotees. Here are the eight main forms, as described in the Puranas:

Asitanga Bhairava: Bestows creative abilities and artistic talents.

Ruru Bhairava: Acts as a divine educator, guiding devotees toward wisdom.

Chanda Bhairava: Grants energy and strength to overcome adversaries.

Krodha Bhairava: Empowers devotees to take bold initiatives.

Unmatta Bhairava: Helps control ego, arrogance, and narcissism.

Kapala Bhairava: Ends fruitless endeavors and unprofitable actions.

Bhishana Bhairava: Nullifies evil influences and negative spirits.

Samhara Bhairava: Dissolves negative karma from past lives.

Additionally, *Swarna Akarshana Bhairava* (Gold-Attracting Bhairava) is a benevolent form associated with wealth and prosperity. Depicted with a red complexion and golden robes, he is believed to bless devotees with financial abundance.

Each form of Bhairav is associated with a specific Shakti (divine feminine energy) and guards one of the 52 Shakti Peeths, sacred sites dedicated to Goddess Shakti across the Indian subcontinent. This connection highlights Bhairav's role as a protector of sacred spaces and a complement to the divine feminine.

Mythological Stories of Kaal Bhairav

The stories of Kaal Bhairav are rooted in ancient Hindu texts like the Shiva Mahapurana, Skanda Purana, and Linga Purana, as well as oral traditions that have been lovingly preserved by priests and devotees. These tales paint a vivid picture of Bhairav Baba as a deity of justice, protection, and spiritual transformation. Let me share some of the most significant mythological stories that define his divine persona.

The Tale of Vaishno Devi and Kaal Bhairav

One of the most beloved stories connecting Kaal Bhairav to another powerful deity is his role in the legend of Vaishno Devi, the revered goddess worshipped in Jammu. This tale, popular in North India, highlights Bhairav's dual nature as both a challenger and a protector.

Long ago, in the Treta Yuga, a young girl named Vaishnavi, an incarnation of Goddess Shakti, was born to fulfill a divine purpose. She was a devout follower of Lord Vishnu but also sought to merge with Lord Shiva through intense meditation. To test her devotion, Lord Shiva sent Kaal

Bhairav, in the form of a fierce Tantric named Bhairavnath, to challenge her resolve.

Bhairavnath, struck by Vaishnavi's beauty and spiritual aura, became obsessed with her and began pursuing her. Vaishnavi, determined to protect her chastity and focus on her penance, fled to the Trikuta Mountains. Bhairavnath chased her relentlessly, unaware that she was a divine incarnation. During her escape, Vaishnavi took refuge in a cave, where she meditated for nine months, transforming into the fierce Goddess Vaishno Devi. When Bhairavnath finally found her, she emerged in her divine form, riding a lion and wielding weapons of divine power. In a fierce battle, she beheaded Bhairavnath, ending his pursuit.

However, as Bhairavnath lay dying, he realized his mistake and sought forgiveness. Moved by his repentance, Vaishno Devi granted him a boon: anyone who visited her shrine in the Trikuta Mountains would also need to pay homage to Bhairavnath to complete their pilgrimage. Thus, a temple dedicated to Bhairav Baba was established near the Vaishno Devi shrine, known as the Bhairavnath Temple. Devotees believe that without offering prayers to Bhairav, their visit to Vaishno Devi remains incomplete.

This story underscores Kaal Bhairav's role as a tester of devotion. While his pursuit of Vaishnavi may seem antagonistic, it was a divine act to strengthen her resolve and reveal her true power. For devotees, this tale teaches that challenges in life are often tests from the divine, meant to lead us toward growth and enlightenment.

The Destruction of Daksha's Yagna

Another powerful myth, briefly touched upon in Part 1, deserves a deeper exploration here. This story, found in the Shiva Mahapurana, showcases Kaal Bhairav's role as a protector of Shiva's honor and a destroyer of arrogance.

Daksha, a powerful king and father of Sati (Shiva's first wife), disapproved of his daughter's marriage to Shiva, whom he considered an uncouth ascetic unfit for royalty. To humiliate Shiva, Daksha organized a grand yagna (sacrificial ritual) and invited all the gods except Shiva and Sati. When Sati attended the yagna against Shiva's wishes, Daksha insulted her and mocked Shiva's divine status. Unable to bear the dishonor, Sati immolated herself in the sacrificial fire, declaring that she would return in another life to marry Shiva again.

When news of Sati's death reached Shiva, his grief turned into uncontrollable rage. From his matted locks, he created two fierce beings: Veerabhadra and Kaal Bhairav. Shiva commanded them to destroy Daksha's yagna and punish those who insulted him. Kaal Bhairav, with his terrifying form, stormed the yagna, wielding a trident and accompanied by his loyal black dog. Together with

Veerabhadra, he wreaked havoc, destroying the sacrificial altar, scattering the gods, and beheading Daksha. The chaos only subsided when the gods pleaded for mercy, and Shiva, moved by their prayers, restored Daksha's life by placing a goat's head on his body.

This story highlights Kaal Bhairav's role as a fierce enforcer of divine justice. It also reflects the theme of loyalty to Shiva, as Bhairav acts as an extension of Shiva's will. For devotees, this tale is a reminder that disrespecting the divine or acting with pride can lead to destruction, but sincere repentance can bring redemption.

The Defeat of Dahurasuran

A lesser-known but significant story from South Indian traditions, particularly in Tamil Nadu, involves Kaal Bhairav's role in defeating the demon Dahurasuran. This tale emphasizes Bhairav's connection to Goddess Kali and his role as a protector of dharma.

Dahurasuran, a powerful demon, had received a boon that he could only be killed by a woman. Empowered by this boon, he terrorized the earth, defying the gods and causing chaos. The gods turned to Goddess Parvati for help. Parvati transformed into her fierce form, Kali, and engaged Dahurasuran in a fierce battle. After slaying the demon, Kali's wrath was so intense that it threatened to consume the world. To calm her, Shiva manifested as a divine child born from Kali's energy. This child merged with Shiva's essence to become Kaal Bhairav, who pacified Kali and restored balance to the universe.

From this union, the Ashta Bhairavas (eight forms of Bhairav) were born, each tasked with guarding a specific direction and protecting devotees from evil. This story highlights Bhairav's origin as a balance between masculine and feminine energies, embodying both Shiva's calmness and Kali's ferocity. In South India, this tale is often recited during festivals like Kalashtami, celebrating Bhairav's protective role.

Tantric Traditions and Kaal Bhairav

Kaal Bhairav holds a special place in Tantric traditions, where he is revered as a deity of immense spiritual power. Tantra, a mystical and esoteric branch of Hinduism, emphasizes the transformation of energies to achieve liberation. Bhairav, as a manifestation of Shiva's primal energy, is central to many Tantric practices, particularly in the Kaula and Aghori sects.

Bhairav in the Cremation Grounds

In Tantric lore, Kaal Bhairav is often associated with cremation grounds, which are considered sacred spaces for spiritual practice. Cremation grounds symbolize the impermanence of life and the dissolution of ego, making them ideal for Tantric sadhana (spiritual practice). Bhairav is believed to reside in these spaces, guarding them and guiding practitioners toward liberation.

One popular Tantric story tells of a yogi named Gorakhnath, a disciple of the great sage Matsyendranath, who sought to master Tantric rituals. To gain spiritual power, Gorakhnath meditated in a cremation ground, invoking Kaal Bhairav. Pleased with his devotion, Bhairav appeared before him, granting him siddhis (spiritual powers) and the ability to transcend fear. This story is often cited in Tantric texts to emphasize Bhairav's role as a guide for those who dare to confront their fears and embrace the divine.

The Role of Liquor in Bhairav Worship

One of the most distinctive aspects of Kaal Bhairav worship in Tantric traditions is the offering of liquor, known as madira or som rasa. In Tantra, liquor symbolizes the nectar of divine consciousness, and offering it to Bhairav is a way to transcend worldly attachments. Devotees believe that Bhairav consumes the liquor spiritually, purifying it and transforming it into prasad (blessed offering). This practice is especially prominent at the Kaal Bhairav Temple in Ujjain, where devotees offer liquor to the deity, and the prasad is distributed to cure ailments and ward off negative energies.

A Tantric legend explains this practice: Once, a group of sages sought to test Kaal Bhairav's power. They offered him a bowl of poisoned liquor, hoping to weaken him. Bhair2av, with his divine wisdom, drank the poison and transformed it into nectar, proving his mastery over life and death. Since then, liquor offerings became a symbol of surrender to Bhairav's divine will, signifying the devotee's willingness to let go of ego and impurities.

Regional Legends and Folktales

Beyond the Puranas and Tantric texts, Kaal Bhairav is the subject of countless regional legends and folktales, especially in Varanasi, Ujjain, and other parts of India. These stories, often shared by priests, locals, and pilgrims, add a personal and relatable dimension to Bhairav's divine presence.

The Miracle of the Black Dog in Varanasi

In Varanasi, a popular folktale tells of a poor farmer named Ramu who lived on the outskirts of the city. Ramu was plagued by a series of misfortunes—his crops failed, his family fell ill, and his debts mounted. Desperate, he visited the Kaal Bhairav Temple and prayed fervently for help. That night, a black dog appeared at his doorstep, refusing to leave. Initially wary, Ramu fed the dog and treated it with kindness, believing it to be a stray.

Over the next few days, Ramu's fortunes began to change. His

crops flourished, his family recovered, and a local merchant offered to clear his debts. One evening, as Ramu sat outside his home, the dog looked at him with knowing eyes and vanished into the darkness. The next day, when Ramu visited the temple to offer thanks, he saw the same dog depicted beside Kaal Bhairav's idol. Overwhelmed, he realized that the dog was none other than Bhairav Baba himself, who had come to protect him. Since then, devotees in Varanasi feed black dogs near the temple, believing them to be manifestations of Kaal Bhairav's divine presence.

This story reflects the belief that Bhairav Baba watches over his devotees, often appearing in humble forms to test their faith and kindness. Feeding black dogs is now a common practice at the Kaal Bhairav Temple, symbolizing devotion and gratitude.

The Haunted Well of Ujjain

In Ujjain, home to another famous Kaal Bhairav Temple, a chilling legend speaks of a haunted well near the temple. Centuries ago, a cruel landlord oppressed the people of Ujjain, exploiting their labor and refusing to pay their wages. A group of villagers, fed up with his tyranny, sought Kaal Bhairav's intervention. They performed a special puja at the temple, offering liquor and chanting the Kaal Bhairav Ashtakam.

That night, the landlord was drawn to a well near the temple by an unseen force. As he peered into the well, he saw a terrifying reflection of Kaal Bhairav, holding a rod of justice. Frightened, he fell into the well and was never seen again. The villagers believed that Kaal Bhairav had punished the landlord for his sins, and the well became known as Bhairav Koop, a site where devotees offer prayers for justice. To this day, visitors to the Ujjain temple avoid looking into the well at night, fearing Bhairav's wrathful gaze.

This tale reinforces Kaal Bhairav's role as Dandapani, the punisher of wrongdoers. It also highlights the temple's significance as a place where devotees seek justice against oppression and injustice.

The Bhairav of Karnataka's Forests

In Karnataka, particularly in the region around Sirsi, a local legend tells of a Bhairav temple hidden deep in the forests. According to the story, a group of hunters once ventured into the jungle, chasing a rare deer. As night fell, they became lost and were surrounded by wild animals. Terrified, they prayed for protection. Suddenly, a fierce figure riding a black dog appeared, driving away the animals and guiding the hunters to safety. The figure revealed himself as Kaal Bhairav and instructed the hunters to build a temple in his honor.

The temple, known as Marikamba Bhairav Temple, became a pilgrimage site for locals, who believe that Kaal Bhairav protects those who venture into dangerous places. This story underscores Bhairav's role as a protector of travelers and those facing peril, a belief that resonates with devotees across India.

The Significance of Kaal Bhairav in Hindu Spirituality

Kaal Bhairav, the fierce guardian of time and justice, holds a unique place in Hinduism. His significance goes beyond his fearsome appearance or his role as a protector; he embodies a profound spiritual truth that resonates with both the common devotee and the philosophical seeker. As I learned more about Bhairav Baba, I realized that his worship is not just about seeking blessings but about understanding life, death, and the eternal cycle of existence.

Master of Time and Mortality

As the deity of Kaal (time), Kaal Bhairav reminds us that time is both a creator and a destroyer. In a world where we often chase fleeting moments, Bhairav Baba teaches the value of discipline, focus, and living in alignment with dharma (righteousness). Devotees believe that praying to Kaal Bhairav helps them manage time wisely, overcome procrastination, and achieve their goals. His mastery over time also makes him a symbol of mortality, urging devotees to confront the impermanence of life and seek spiritual liberation (moksha).

In Varanasi, known as the city of liberation, Kaal Bhairav's role as

the Kotwal of Kashi is paramount. It is said that he guards the spiritual boundaries of the city, ensuring that those who die in Kashi attain moksha. This belief draws countless pilgrims to the Kaal Bhairav Temple, seeking his blessings to transcend the cycle of birth and death. For many, Bhairav Baba is a bridge between the material and spiritual worlds, guiding them toward eternal freedom.

Protector Against Evil

Kaal Bhairav's fierce form, with his trident, skull garland, and loyal black dog, makes him a powerful protector against evil forces. Devotees turn to him to ward off black magic, evil spirits, and negative energies. In a world filled with uncertainties, Bhairav Baba offers a sense of security, shielding his devotees from harm. This protective aspect is especially significant in Tantric traditions, where Bhairav is invoked to neutralize malevolent forces and purify the spiritual environment.

Stories abound of devotees who were saved from misfortune after praying at the Kaal Bhairav Temple. Whether it's protection from enemies, recovery from illness, or overcoming financial struggles, Bhairav Baba is seen as a divine warrior who fights for his devotees. His epithet Dandapani (one who holds a rod to punish sinners) underscores his role as an enforcer of justice, ensuring that wrongdoers face consequences while the righteous are rewarded.

A Guide to Spiritual Transformation

For spiritual seekers, Kaal Bhairav represents the courage to face fear, particularly the fear of death. His association with cremation grounds, a place where life meets its end, symbolizes the dissolution of ego and attachment. In Tantric and Shaivite traditions, Bhairav is seen as a guide to transcendence, helping devotees move beyond worldly desires to realize their divine nature.

In Kashmir Shaivism, as taught by the philosopher Abhinavagupta, Bhairav is not just a deity but a state of consciousness. The Vijnana Bhairava Tantra describes him as the embodiment of pure awareness, where the duality of creation and destruction merges into oneness. This philosophical perspective makes Bhairav worship appealing to those seeking deeper spiritual insights, offering a path to self-realization through meditation and surrender.

A Symbol of Balance

Bhairav Baba's dual nature—fierce yet compassionate, destructive yet protective—makes him a symbol of balance. He teaches devotees to embrace both the light and dark aspects of life, recognizing that destruction is often a precursor to creation. His stories, such as the beheading of Brahma or the protection of Vaishno Devi, highlight the need for humility, justice, and devotion. For the common person, Bhairav Baba is a reminder that life's challenges are opportunities for growth, and his blessings can transform even the darkest moments into light.

Rituals and Festivals of Kaal Bhairav Worship

The worship of Kaal Bhairav is steeped in rituals that reflect his fierce and Tantric nature. These practices, performed with devotion and reverence, are a way for devotees to connect with Bhairav Baba and seek his blessings. At the Kaal Bhairav Temple in Varanasi and other temples across India, these rituals are vibrant, colorful, and deeply meaningful. Let me share the key rituals and festivals that bring Bhairav Baba's presence to life.

Daily Worship at the Kaal Bhairav Temple

The Kaal Bhairav Temple in Varanasi is a bustling hub of devotion, with daily rituals that draw devotees from all walks of life. The day begins with the Mangala Aarti, a pre-dawn ritual where priests offer lamps, incense, and prayers to awaken the deity. The idol of Kaal Bhairav, with its silver face adorned with a garland of skulls, is bathed with water, milk, and sometimes liquor, symbolizing purification and surrender.

Devotees offer a variety of items to Bhairav Baba, reflecting his unique preferences:

Liquor: One of the most distinctive offerings, liquor (often country-made or desi daru) is poured into a small bowl placed before the idol. Devotees believe that Bhairav spiritually consumes the offering, transforming it into prasad that heals ailments and wards off evil. This practice is especially prominent at the Kaal Bhairav Temple in Ujjain, where the deity is said to "drink" the liquor through the idol's mouth, a phenomenon considered miraculous.

Paan and Betel Nut: Paan leaves, betel nuts, and cloves are offered as symbols of hospitality and respect, believed to please Bhairav Baba.

Meat Offerings: In some regions, particularly in Tantric traditions, non-vegetarian offerings like meat or fish are made, especially during special festivals. These offerings are later distributed as prasad or offered to the poor.

Mustard Oil Lamps: Lighting mustard oil lamps (diyas) is a common practice, believed to dispel negativity and attract Bhairav's protection. Devotees often light 11 or 21 lamps as part of their prayers.

Black Dogs: Feeding black dogs near the temple is a cherished ritual, as they are considered Bhairav's vahana (vehicle). Devotees offer rotis, rice, or sweets to stray dogs, believing that this act pleases the deity.

The temple priests chant mantras like the Kaal Bhairav Ashtakam, a hymn composed by Adi Shankaracharya, which praises Bhairav's power and seeks his blessings. Another powerful mantra is the Beej Mantra of Kaal Bhairav: "Om Hreem Batukaya Apaduddharanaya Kuru Kuru Batukaya Hreem". Devotees recite this mantra 108 times, often using a rudraksha mala, to invoke Bhairav's protection and remove obstacles.

Major Festivals

Two festivals dedicated to Kaal Bhairav are celebrated with great fervor: Bhairava Ashtami and Kalashtami. These occasions bring thousands of devotees to the Kaal Bhairav Temple, transforming it into a vibrant center of devotion.

Bhairava Ashtami

Celebrated on the eighth day of the waning moon (Krishna Paksha Ashtami) in the month of Margashirsha (November–December), Bhairava Ashtami marks the appearance day of Kaal Bhairav. The temple is decorated with flowers, lights, and colorful rangolis. Special pujas are conducted, including the Havan (fire ritual) and Abhishekam (ritual bathing of the idol). Devotees fast, chant mantras, and offer liquor, paan, and sweets. A grand procession, with the deity's idol carried through the streets, is a highlight in some regions. It is believed that worshipping Bhairav on this day removes fear, grants protection, and fulfills desires.

Kalashtami

Observed monthly on the eighth day of the waning moon, Kalashtami is dedicated to Kaal Bhairav. While less elaborate than Bhairava Ashtami, it is a significant day for devotees to visit the temple, offer prayers, and seek blessings for overcoming obstacles. Many perform special Tantric rituals, including chanting the Kaal Bhairav Ashtakam and offering liquor or mustard oil lamps. In Varanasi, the temple sees a steady stream of devotees on

Kalashtami, especially those seeking protection from enemies or spiritual afflictions.

Tantric Rituals

In Tantric traditions, Kaal Bhairav worship involves more esoteric practices, often performed by trained practitioners under the guidance of a guru. These rituals are conducted in cremation grounds or secluded spaces, emphasizing Bhairav's connection to transformation and liberation. Common Tantric practices include:

Sadhana with Mantras: Reciting specific mantras, such as the Batuk Bhairav Mantra, for 21 days to gain spiritual powers or
siddhis.

Yantra Worship: Using a Bhairav Yantra (a mystical diagram) to meditate and invoke the deity's energy.

Offerings of Five Elements: Presenting the Panchamakara (five Tantric offerings—wine, meat, fish, grains, and union) to symbolize the transcendence of worldly attachments.

These rituals require strict discipline and purity of intention, as Bhairav is believed to respond only to sincere devotees. Misuse of Tantric practices is said to invite his wrath, reinforcing his role as a deity of justice.

The Modern-Day Scene of Kaal Bhairav Worship

In today's fast-paced world, the Kaal Bhairav Temple in Varanasi remains a spiritual anchor, drawing devotees from across India and beyond. Its narrow lanes, filled with the aroma of flowers and the sound of chants, are a testament to Bhairav Baba's enduring relevance. But the worship of Kaal Bhairav is not limited to Varanasi; it has spread to urban and rural India, adapting to modern sensibilities while retaining its traditional essence.

The Kaal Bhairav Temple in Varanasi Today

Walking through the Vishwanath Gali in Varanasi, you can't miss the Kaal Bhairav Temple, its ancient stone walls standing tall amidst the chaos of the city. The temple is a melting pot of devotees—locals seeking protection, pilgrims completing their Kashi yatra, and tourists intrigued by its mystique. The idol of Kaal Bhairav, with its silver face and intense eyes, is a focal point of devotion, often covered with a cloth except during major festivals.

The temple's daily routine is a blend of tradition and accessibility. Priests perform aartis multiple times a day, and devotees line up to offer liquor, paan, and flowers. The practice of feeding black dogs remains popular, with vendors selling rotis and sweets for this purpose. The temple is especially crowded on Sundays, Tuesdays, and Kalashtami days, when devotees believe Bhairav's blessings are most potent.

In recent years, the temple has embraced modern technology. Live aartis are streamed online, allowing devotees worldwide to participate virtually. The temple's trust maintains a website with information on rituals, festivals, and donation options, making it easier for younger generations to stay connected. Yet, the essence of the temple remains unchanged—its sanctity lies in its simplicity and the unwavering faith of its devotees.

Other Kaal Bhairav Temples

While the Varanasi temple is the most famous, other Kaal Bhairav temples across India hold their own significance, each with unique practices:

Kaal Bhairav Temple, Ujjain

Located in Madhya Pradesh, this temple is renowned for its liquor offerings. Devotees pour liquor into a bowl, and the idol is said to "drink" it, a phenomenon that draws crowds of curious visitors. The temple is part of the Ujjain pilgrimage circuit, alongside the Mahakaleshwar Temple, and is especially busy during Mahashivratri and Bhairava Ashtami.

Bhairav Temple, Delhi

The Ashta Bhairav Temple in Delhi, near Purana Qila, is dedicated to the eight forms of Bhairav. It is a serene spot where devotees perform simple rituals like lighting lamps and chanting mantras. The temple's peaceful ambiance contrasts with Varanasi's bustling energy, attracting urban devotees seeking solace.

Marikamba Bhairav Temple, Karnataka

In Sirsi, Karnataka, this temple is revered for its connection to the forest legend mentioned in Part 2. Devotees offer coconuts and flowers, and the temple hosts vibrant fairs during Bhairava Ashtami, drawing rural communities together.

These temples reflect the widespread devotion to Kaal Bhairav, adapting to regional cultures while maintaining core rituals like liquor offerings and dog-feeding.

Bhairav Worship in Modern India

In urban India, Bhairav worship has found a place among diverse groups, from professionals seeking success to students praying for focus. Small Bhairav shrines are common in cities like Mumbai, Kolkata, and Bangalore, often tucked into busy markets or residential areas. Social media has amplified his presence, with pages and groups dedicated to sharing Bhairav mantras, stories, and festival updates.

The Tantric aspect of Bhairav worship, once limited to secluded practitioners, has gained interest among spiritual seekers exploring yoga and meditation. Workshops on Tantric mantras and Bhairav sadhana are offered in urban centers, blending ancient practices with modern spirituality. However, priests emphasize the need for proper guidance, as Bhairav's energy is powerful and demands respect.

Globally, the Indian diaspora has carried Bhairav worship to countries like the USA, Canada, and the UK, where small shrines and community pujas keep the tradition alive.

Online platforms like YouTube host recordings of the Kaal Bhairav Ashtakam, allowing devotees to connect with the deity from afar.

Kaal Bhairav is not just a deity of mythology but a living force that guides devotees through life's challenges. His stories, from the beheading of Brahma to the protection of Vaishno Devi, teach us humility, justice, and the courage to face our fears. His rituals, from liquor offerings to chanting mantras, create a bridge between the human and the divine. And his temples, especially the Kaal Bhairav Temple in Varanasi, stand as eternal reminders of his role as the guardian of time and dharma.

For the common person, Bhairav Baba is a protector who shields against evil and grants strength in times of need. For the spiritual seeker, he is a guide to liberation, helping dissolve the ego and embrace the divine. In today's world, where uncertainty and change are constant, Bhairav Baba's teachings remain relevant, urging us to live with purpose, discipline, and devotion.

The Legend of CharBhuja Nath

In the heart of Rajasthan, where the sands whisper ancient tales and the Aravali hills stand as silent guardians, lies the sacred land of Mewar, a region steeped in devotion and valor. Among its many divine stories, one shines brightly, etched into the hearts of the people—the legend of Charbhuja Nath, the four-armed Lord Vishnu, whose temple in the village of Garhbor stands as a beacon of faith. This is not just a story of a deity but a saga of miracles, courage, and the unbreakable bond between the divine and the devotees.

The Origins of Charbhuja Nath

Long ago, in the time when gods walked closer to the earth and the line between the mortal and divine was thin, the land of Mewar was a tapestry of kingdoms and clans. The Rajputs, known for their bravery and honor, ruled these lands, but their hearts were anchored in devotion to the divine. Among the many gods they worshipped, Lord Vishnu, the preserver of the universe, held a special place. It is said that in the 15th century, during the reign of the Sisodia dynasty, a miracle unfolded that would forever change the spiritual landscape of Rajasthan.

In the village of Garhbor, nestled in the Rajsamand district, lived a simple yet devout community of farmers, artisans, and warriors. Among them was a man named Gangadas, a humble devotee of Lord Vishnu. Gangadas was no ordinary man; his heart was a temple of faith, and his days were spent in prayer and service. The villagers revered him for his wisdom and kindness, but none could have foreseen the divine destiny awaiting him.

One serene morning, as the first rays of the sun kissed the fields, Gangadas set out to plow his land near the banks of the Gomti River. The air was filled with the scent of earth and the songs of birds, and Gangadas felt a strange pull in his heart, as if the divine was calling him. As his plow cut through the soil, it struck something hard—a stone, he thought at first. But as he knelt to clear the earth, his hands uncovered a magnificent idol, its four arms gleaming under the morning light. The idol was none other than Lord Vishnu, adorned with a conch, discus, mace, and lotus, his serene face radiating divine grace.

Gangadas fell to his knees, overwhelmed by awe and reverence. The villagers gathered, their eyes wide with wonder, as the news spread like wildfire. The idol, they believed, was no ordinary statue—it was Charbhuja Nath, the four-armed Lord, who had chosen to reveal himself to his devotees. The elders recalled ancient prophecies from the Puranas, which spoke of Vishnu manifesting in times of need to guide and protect his people. This, they declared, was a sign that the Lord had come to bless Mewar and its people.

The discovery of the idol was not just a moment of joy but a call to action. The villagers, led by Gangadas, decided to build a temple to enshrine Charbhuja Nath. They toiled day and night, their hands guided by devotion, crafting a sanctuary worthy of the Lord. The temple, simple yet majestic, became a place where the divine and mortal could meet. The idol was installed with great ceremony, and priests chanted verses from the Vedas and Puranas, invoking Vishnu's blessings. From that day, the temple of Charbhuja Nath became a sacred pilgrimage site, drawing devotees from far and wide.

The Warrior's Faith: The Role of the Rajputs

The story of Charbhuja Nath is deeply intertwined with the valor of the Rajputs, particularly the Sisodia rulers of Mewar. During the 15th century, Mewar was a land of constant battles, as rival kingdoms and invaders sought to claim its riches. The Sisodia kings, known for their unyielding courage, often turned to divine intervention to protect their people. Among them was Rana Kumbha, a legendary ruler whose reign (1433–1468 CE) marked a golden era for Mewar.

Rana Kumbha was not only a warrior but also a devout follower of Vishnu. When news of the miraculous idol reached his court, he saw it as a divine omen. He visited Garhbor, where he offered his obeisance to Charbhuja Nath and declared the temple a royal sanctuary. The Rana believed that the Lord's four arms symbolized strength, wisdom, protection, and prosperity—qualities essential for a ruler. He vowed to seek Charbhuja Nath's blessings before every battle, and it is said that the Lord never failed him.

One of the most famous legends associated with Charbhuja

Nath involves Rana Kumbha's victory at the Battle of Kumbhalgarh. The fortress of Kumbhalgarh, built under his patronage, was a marvel of architecture, but it faced a fierce siege by a coalition of rival kings. Outnumbered and surrounded, Rana Kumbha turned to Charbhuja Nath for strength. He spent the night in prayer at the temple, offering his sword and shield to the Lord. As dawn broke, a divine vision appeared to him—a radiant figure of Vishnu, assuring him of victory. Inspired, the Rana led his forces with unmatched courage, and against all odds, they repelled the invaders. The victory was attributed to Charbhuja Nath, and the temple's fame grew as a place where faith could move mountains.

The Rajputs' devotion to Charbhuja Nath extended beyond battles. The temple became a center of cultural and spiritual life, where festivals, music, and dance flourished. The Sisodia kings endowed the temple with lands and riches, ensuring its upkeep. The priests, known as Bhopas, sang ballads of the Lord's miracles, preserving the stories for generations. These ballads, part of Rajasthan's rich oral tradition, became a bridge between the divine and the common people, making Charbhuja Nath a household name.

The Temple and Its Traditions

The Charbhuja Nath temple in Garhbor is a marvel of Rajasthani architecture. Built in the Nagara style, its spire rises like a prayer to the heavens, adorned with intricate carvings of gods, goddesses, and celestial beings. The sanctum sanctorum houses the idol of Charbhuja Nath, crafted from black marble, its four arms a striking reminder of Vishnu's divine attributes. The idol's eyes, said to be carved with such skill that they seem alive, draw devotees into a trance of devotion.

The temple is a hub of activity, especially during festivals like Janmashtami and Navratri. Janmashtami, the birth of Lord Krishna (an avatar of Vishnu), is celebrated with grandeur. The idol is bathed in milk and adorned with jewels, and the temple echoes with bhajans and kirtans. Devotees fast, dance, and reenact scenes from Krishna's life, believing that Charbhuja Nath embodies the playful spirit of the divine cowherd.

Navratri sees the temple transform into a vibrant tapestry of colors. Women perform the Garba and Dandiya dances, their swirling skirts mirroring the cosmic dance of the universe. The temple fair, or mela, draws thousands, with stalls selling sweets, toys, and religious trinkets. The air is thick with the aroma of jalebis and the sound of folk songs praising the Lord.

One unique tradition is the offering of "chhappan bhog," a feast of 56 dishes presented to Charbhuja Nath. This ritual, rooted in the belief that Vishnu loves variety, includes everything from savory kachoris to sweet laddoos. After the offering, the food is distributed as prasad, ensuring that no devotee leaves hungry.

The temple also hosts the recitation of the Vishnu Sahasranama, the thousand names of Vishnu, believed to cleanse the soul and grant wishes. The Bhopas, hereditary priests, play a vital role, narrating the Lord's stories through Phad paintings—colorful scrolls that depict the deity's miracles. These paintings, a hallmark of Rajasthani culture, are carried from village to village, spreading the legend of Charbhuja Nath.

Legends and Beliefs

The story of Charbhuja Nath is not just about a deity or a temple; it's a reflection of Rajasthan's soul. The four arms of the Lord are said to symbolize the four pillars of dharma: truth, righteousness, compassion, and devotion. Devotees believe that worshipping Charbhuja Nath strengthens these virtues, guiding them through life's challenges.

One popular belief is that the idol is swayambhu—self-manifested—and not crafted by human hands. This adds to its sanctity, as it's seen as a direct gift from Vishnu. Elders tell of a time when the idol was threatened by invaders who sought to destroy Hindu temples. Yet, each time, the attackers were struck by mysterious ailments or fled in fear, convinced that the Lord himself protected his abode.

Another legend ties Charbhuja Nath to the Pandavas of the Mahabharata. It is said that during their exile, the Pandavas visited Mewar and worshipped at a sacred spot near Garhbor. Kunti, their mother, prayed to Vishnu for protection, and the Lord blessed her with strength. Some believe that the idol of Charbhuja Nath was hidden underground during those ancient times, only to be revealed centuries later to Gangadas.

The temple is also linked to the Nath sect, a group of yogis who worship Shiva and Vishnu. Some stories suggest that a Nath yogi, meditating near Garhbor, had a vision of Vishnu, who instructed him to protect the idol until it was discovered. This connection adds a mystical layer to the temple's history, blending Shaivism and Vaishnavism in a uniquely Rajasthani way.

The Legacy of Charbhuja Nath

As centuries passed, the fame of Charbhuja Nath spread beyond Rajasthan. Pilgrims from Gujarat, Madhya Pradesh, and even distant corners of India visit Garhbor, seeking the Lord's blessings. The temple has weathered invasions, famines, and the passage of time, yet its sanctity remains untouched. The Sisodia kings are gone, but their devotion lives on in the hearts of the people.

Today, the temple is not just a religious site but a cultural landmark. It inspires poets, artists, and musicians, who draw from its stories to create works that celebrate

Rajasthan's heritage. The annual fairs continue to draw crowds, blending spirituality with community spirit. For the people of Mewar, Charbhuja Nath is more than a deity—he is a friend, a protector, and a guide.

The story of Charbhuja Nath reminds us that faith can transform lives. From Gangadas's humble discovery to Rana Kumbha's victories, from Meera's miracle to Lakshman's salvation, the Lord's presence has been a constant source of hope. In a world that often feels uncertain, the temple stands as a reminder that the divine is never far, ready to listen to those who call with a pure heart.

A Call to the Faithful

As the sun sets over Garhbor, casting a golden glow on the temple's spire, the air fills with the sound of bells and the fragrance of incense. Devotees, young and old, gather to offer their prayers, their faces alight with faith. The story of Charbhuja Nath is not just a tale of the past but a living tradition, carried forward by every heart that beats in devotion.

So, come to Garhbor, walk the sacred paths, and feel the presence of the four-armed Lord. Whether you seek strength, peace, or simply a moment of connection with the divine, Charbhuja Nath awaits. His story, woven from the threads of history, myth, and belief, is a testament to the enduring power of faith—a power that continues to light the way for generations.

The Legend of Sanwaliya Seth Mandir, Mandaphia

The Beginning: A Sacred Land Awakens

In the heart of Rajasthan, where the rugged hills of Chittorgarh meet the dusty plains, lies a small village called Mandaphia. It's a place that hums with a quiet energy, as if the earth itself holds secrets of the divine. The air carries the scent of desert flowers, and the distant clang of temple bells echoes through the valleys. This is the home of Sanwaliya Seth Mandir, a sacred shrine dedicated to Lord Krishna, known here as Sanwaliya Seth, the dark-complexioned lord who is both a divine protector and a partner in prosperity. This temple is no ordinary place of worship. It's a beacon of hope, a court where wishes are granted, and a sanctuary where the faithful find solace.

Long ago, in a time when the land of Mewar was steeped in tales of valor, devotion, and sacrifice, Mandaphia was a quiet hamlet nestled between the villages of Bhadsoda and Chapar, about 40 kilometers from the historic city of Chittorgarh. The year was 1840, and the region was a tapestry of fields, acacia trees, and simple lives. The people of Mandaphia were farmers and herders, their days filled with the rhythm of the seasons and their nights with stories of gods and heroes. Little did they know that their village was about to become a sacred destination, touched by the hand of Lord Krishna himself.

This is the story of how Sanwaliya Seth Mandir came to be—a tale woven from the threads of Hindu mythology, local legends, and the unshakable faith of millions. It's a story of divine dreams, miraculous idols, and a temple that became a symbol of Krishna's boundless love and generosity. Let me take you back to that fateful moment when the divine chose Mandaphia to reveal its presence.

The Divine Dream: The Call of Sanwaliya Seth

It was a warm summer night in 1840, under a sky glittering with stars, when a milkman named Bholaram Gurjar fell into a deep sleep in his modest home in Mandaphia. Bholaram was a simple man, known for his honesty and devotion. He tended his cows, cared for his family, and lived a life of quiet faith, always offering a prayer to Lord Krishna before his day began. That night, as the world around him slept, Bholaram's dreams were filled with a radiant vision.

In his dream, a figure appeared, cloaked in divine light. It was Lord Krishna, his dark skin shimmering like a moonless night, his eyes twinkling with mischief and kindness. He wore a peacock feather crown, and his flute rested gently in his hands. "Bholaram," Krishna said in a voice that was both gentle and commanding, "beneath the earth in Chapar village, near the old acacia tree, lie three idols of mine. They are waiting to be found. Dig them out, and let my presence bless this land."

Bholaram awoke with a start, his heart pounding. The dream felt more real than anything he had ever experienced. He could still hear Krishna's voice, feel the warmth of his presence. Without wasting a moment, he gathered a few trusted villagers and shared his vision. Some were skeptical, but Bholaram's sincerity convinced them to follow him to the spot he had seen in his dream—a barren patch of land near Chapar, marked by a gnarled acacia tree that stood like a sentinel.

As the villagers began to dig, their spades struck something hard. The earth gave way, revealing three magnificent idols of Lord Krishna, each one breathtakingly beautiful. Their dark, glossy surfaces gleamed in the sunlight, and their serene expressions seemed to radiate divine energy. The villagers gasped, falling to their knees in awe. These were no ordinary statues—they were alive with the presence of Krishna himself.

The discovery sparked a wave of excitement. The village elders, led by Rodulalji Jain, the headman of Mandaphia, gathered to decide what to do with the idols. After much discussion, they agreed that each idol deserved a home. One was kept at Chapar, where it was found, and a temple was built at the very spot, known as the Prakatya Sthal, the place of divine appearance. The second idol was taken to Bhadsoda, a nearby village, where another temple was established. The third, and most beautiful, idol was brought to Mandaphia with great fanfare, accompanied by chants of "Jai Sanwaliya Seth!" The villagers carried it in a procession, their hearts swelling with joy, and placed it temporarily in the home of Bholaram Gurjar, in a small courtyard known as Parende.

This idol, it is said, was the same one that had once captivated the heart of Meera Bai, the legendary devotee of Krishna. Meera, the poetess-princess of Mewar, was known for her ecstatic devotion, dancing and singing bhajans in praise of her beloved Girdhar Gopal. Local legend holds that this very idol was part of the entourage of saints and sages with whom Meera traveled, carrying Krishna's presence wherever she went. Now, centuries later, it had found a new home in Mandaphia, ready to bless the faithful once more. The villagers, under Rodulalji's guidance, built a small temple with four walls and a simple roof to house the idol. They performed the necessary rituals, chanting mantras and offering flowers, milk, and sweets. The temple was modest, but its sanctity was undeniable. Word of the miraculous discovery spread quickly, and soon, devotees from across Mewar began flocking to Mandaphia to seek the blessings of Sanwaliya Seth, the dark lord who fulfilled every heart's desire.

The Legend of Sanwaliya Seth

The name "Sanwaliya Seth" carries a special meaning. "Sanwaliya" refers to Krishna's dark, radiant complexion, a symbol of his divine beauty. "Seth" means a wealthy merchant or partner, reflecting the unique bond that devotees share with this form of Krishna. In Mandaphia,

Sanwaliya Seth is not just a deity to worship but a partner in life's endeavors, especially in matters of prosperity and business. This belief stems from a beautiful legend tied to Krishna's childhood friend, Sudama.

Long ago, in the ancient city of Dwarka, Sudama, a poor Brahmin and Krishna's dear friend, visited his divine companion. Sudama's family was starving, and he arrived at Krishna's palace with nothing but a handful of puffed rice as a gift. Krishna, the lord of the universe, welcomed Sudama with open arms, treating him with the warmth of a brother. Rukmini, Krishna's wife, prepared a feast of 55 dishes, but Sudama hesitated, thinking of his hungry wife and children back home. Overcome with emotion, he sat under a tree, unable to eat.

At that moment, a miracle unfolded. In Sudama's village, a bullock cart filled with poori and kheer appeared, and a voice announced, "A grandson has been born to Sanwaliya Seth!" The villagers were invited to a grand puja, and Sudama's family was fed abundantly. When Sudama returned home, he found his humble hut transformed into a grand home, his family blessed with wealth and happiness. This story gave rise to the name "Sanwaliya Seth," symbolizing Krishna's role as a generous partner who shares prosperity with his devotees.

In Mandaphia, this legend shapes the way people worship Sanwaliya Seth. Many devotees, especially traders and businessmen, consider him their business partner, offering a share of their income to the temple as a gesture of gratitude. They believe that by including Sanwaliya Seth in their ventures, their wealth multiplies, and their hardships vanish. This unique relationship has made the temple a magnet for those seeking financial stability and success.

The Miracles: Tales of Faith and Fulfillment

The Sanwaliya Seth Mandir is a place where miracles are not just stories but lived experiences. One of the most famous tales dates back to 1992, when Bhairon Singh Shekhawat, the then Chief Minister of Rajasthan, visited Mandaphia. The temple's darshan hours are strictly observed, closing from 12 noon to 2:30 p.m. Shekhawat arrived at 2 p.m., eager to have darshan of Sanwaliya Seth. The priests were summoned, and they tried to open the lock on the sanctum sanctorum. Despite their efforts, the lock refused to budge. The crowd grew restless, but at exactly 2:30 p.m., the same key turned effortlessly, and the doors swung open. The devotees erupted in cheers, seeing this as a miracle of Sanwaliya Seth's divine will. Shekhawat, deeply moved, offered his prayers and left with a heart full of reverence.

Another story tells of a merchant named Rameshwar from Udaipur, who visited the temple in the 1970s. Rameshwar's business was failing, and he was on the verge of bankruptcy. In despair, he heard of Sanwaliya Seth's reputation as a partner in prosperity. He traveled to Mandaphia, offered a small portion of his remaining wealth, and vowed to share a percentage of his future earnings with the temple. Within months, his business began to recover. Orders poured in, debts were cleared, and Rameshwar's shop became one of the most prosperous in the city. True to his word, he returned to Mandaphia every month, offering a share of his profits to Sanwaliya Seth. His story spread, inspiring countless others to seek the lord's blessings.

The Rituals: A Dance of Devotion

The Sanwaliya Seth Mandir is a place of vibrant rituals, each one steeped in tradition and meaning. The temple opens its doors at 5:30 a.m. with the Mangla Aarti, a morning prayer that fills the air with the sound of bells and bhajans. Devotees gather to witness the idol of Sanwaliya Seth, adorned with garlands, silks, and jewels, his dark form glowing under the lamplight. The aarti is a moment of connection, where the faithful feel Krishna's presence in their hearts.

Throughout the day, devotees offer milk, curd, ghee, and sweets like peda and laddoo, which are considered Krishna's favorites. The temple's priests perform these offerings with care, chanting mantras that echo through the sanctum. The prasad is distributed among the devotees, believed to carry Sanwaliya Seth's blessings. Unlike some temples, the prasad here is not taken home but consumed on the premises, a practice rooted in the belief that it absorbs the divine energy of the temple.

One of the most significant rituals is the offering of a share of one's income. Businessmen and traders often bring a portion of their earnings—sometimes a fixed percentage, like one-tenth—as a tribute to Sanwaliya Seth, their divine partner. The temple's donation box, placed near the sanctum, overflows with offerings, a testament to the devotees' faith in Krishna's generosity. It's said that the temple's treasury has grown so vast that it rivals the wealth of some small towns, with crores of rupees and kilograms of gold and silver offered each year.

Festivals like Janmashtami, Krishna's birthday, transform Mandaphia into a sea of devotion. The temple is decorated with flowers, lights, and colorful fabrics, and the air is filled with bhajans and kirtans. Devotees fast, sing, and dance, celebrating the birth of their beloved Girdhar Gopal. Other festivals, like Holi and Ekadashi, also draw massive crowds, with the temple becoming a focal point for spiritual and cultural celebrations.

The temple has strict rules to maintain its sanctity. Darshan is closed from 12 noon to 2:30 p.m., a time when Krishna is believed to rest. Photography inside the sanctum is forbidden, as it's thought to disrupt the divine energy. Devotees are also advised to approach the temple with a pure heart, free from deceit, as Sanwaliya Seth is believed to see through all pretense.

The Connection to Meera Bai

The Sanwaliya Seth Mandir holds a special place in the hearts of devotees because of its connection to Meera Bai, the poetess-saint whose love for Krishna is legendary. Meera lived in the 16th century, a time of great turmoil in Mewar. Born a princess, she renounced her royal life to dedicate herself to Krishna, whom she called Girdhar Gopal. Her bhajans, filled with longing and devotion, are still sung across India.

According to local legend, the idol of Sanwaliya Seth in Mandaphia is the same one that Meera worshipped. It's said that Meera traveled with a group of saints and sages, carrying sacred idols of Krishna. During the invasions of Aurangzeb, these idols were hidden underground to protect them from desecration. An acacia tree grew over the spot in Chapar, marking the location until Bholaram's dream revealed it centuries later. When the idol was brought to Mandaphia, devotees recognized it as Meera's Girdhar Gopal, the lord who inspired her ecstatic dances and soulful bhajans.

This connection adds a layer of mystique to the temple. Devotees believe that by worshipping Sanwaliya Seth, they are touching the same divine presence that moved Meera to write, "Mere to Girdhar Gopal, doosro na koi" ("My only beloved is Girdhar Gopal, there is no other"). Her spirit lingers in Mandaphia, and many feel her presence during the temple's bhajans and kirtans, as if she is still singing to her beloved Krishna.

A Land of Valor and Faith

To understand the significance of Sanwaliya Seth Mandir, we must look at the historical tapestry of Mewar. Chittorgarh, just 40 kilometers away, is a city of legends, known for its massive fort and tales of Rajput bravery. In the 16th century, Mewar was ruled by Rana Sanga, a warrior king who fought against Babur. His son, Bhojraj, was Meera Bai's husband, but their marriage was short-lived, as Bhojraj died young. Meera's parents also passed away, leaving her alone in a world of political upheaval.

During this time, a group of saints and sages roamed Mewar, carrying sacred idols of Krishna. One such group, led by a saint named Dayaram, is believed to have possessed the idols that later became Sanwaliya Seth. To protect them from invaders, the idols were buried in Chapar, where they remained hidden for centuries. The village of Bhadsoda, near Mandaphia, also has a rich history, tied to Pritha, the sister of Prithviraj Chauhan, who was married to Rana Samar Singh of Chittor. The region was a melting pot of devotion and courage, and the emergence of Sanwaliya Seth's idols in 1840 was seen as a divine reaffirmation of Mewar's spiritual legacy.

The temple's growth reflects the region's prosperity. In 1956, the Shree Sanwaliyaji Mandir Prabandhakarini Committee was formed, a trust of 65 members from 16 nearby villages, including Mandaphia. This trust oversaw the temple's development, transforming the simple structure into a grand edifice. By 1961–62, a pucca temple replaced the original mud structure, and in the 1980s, intricate glasswork was added, making the temple a visual marvel. In 1991, the Rajasthan government took over the temple's management, establishing the Shree Sanwaliyaji Mandir Mandal, which continues to oversee its operations.

The Beliefs: A Bond of Trust and Prosperity

The Sanwaliya Seth Mandir is more than a place of worship; it's a symbol of trust and partnership. The core belief is that Sanwaliya Seth fulfills the wishes of those who approach him with a pure heart. Whether it's success in business, healing from illness, or harmony in the family, devotees believe that Krishna, as Sanwaliya Seth, listens to every prayer.

The temple's reputation as a "business partner" is unique. Many devotees, especially merchants and traders, dedicate a portion of their income to Sanwaliya Seth, believing that he multiplies their wealth. This practice is rooted in the legend of Sudama, where Krishna's generosity transformed a poor man's life. The temple's donation box is a testament to this belief, with offerings of cash, gold, and silver pouring in daily. In recent years, the temple's treasury has reported crores of rupees and kilograms of precious metals, a sign of the devotees' faith and gratitude.

Another belief is that Sanwaliya Seth protects against financial hardship. Devotees who visit the temple regularly claim that they never face poverty, as Krishna ensures their prosperity. This belief has made the temple a magnet for businessmen from across Rajasthan and beyond, who see Sanwaliya Seth as a divine ally in their ventures.

The temple is also associated with Meera Bai's devotion, and many believe that her spirit blesses those who sing her bhajans. During festivals, the air is filled with her songs, and devotees feel a deep connection to her ecstatic love for Krishna. The temple's dark idol, believed to be Meera's Girdhar Gopal, is seen as a living presence, capable of responding to the faithful.

A Journey to Krishna's Court

Today, Sanwaliya Seth Mandir is one of Rajasthan's most revered pilgrimage sites, drawing lakhs of devotees each year. Located on the Chittorgarh–Udaipur Highway, it's easily accessible, about 40 kilometers from Chittorgarh and 80 kilometers from Udaipur. The nearest railway station is Chittorgarh, 33 kilometers away, with regular trains from cities like Jaipur, Delhi, and Mumbai. The Maharana Pratap Airport in Udaipur, 58 kilometers away, serves those traveling by air. Buses and taxis ply regularly, making the temple a convenient destination for pilgrims.

The temple's architecture is a blend of traditional Rajasthani style and modern grandeur. Its pillared halls, carved domes, and intricate glasswork create a mesmerizing atmosphere. The idol of Sanwaliya Seth, adorned with jewels and silks, is the focal point, its dark form radiating serenity and power. The temple is open from 5:30 a.m. to 12 p.m. and 2:30 p.m. to 11 p.m., with the morning aarti being the best time for a peaceful darshan.

The surrounding area is rich with history and spirituality. The Chittorgarh Fort, a UNESCO World Heritage Site, is just an hour away, with its tales of Rajput valor and Meera Bai's devotion. The Meera Temple within the fort is a must-visit for those inspired by her legacy. Nathdwara, home to the Shreenathji Temple, is 85 kilometers away, making it a popular stop for devotees combining their pilgrimage with a visit to another major Krishna shrine.

The temple offers facilities like guesthouses, such as the Sanwariya Dham Guest House, and dining halls that serve simple, vegetarian meals. Festivals like Janmashtami and Holi see the temple at its most vibrant, with thousands gathering to celebrate. The temple's YouTube channel offers live darshan, allowing devotees worldwide to connect with Sanwaliya Seth.

The Legacy: A Light of Faith

This is a place where dreams come true, where the poor become prosperous, and where the faithful find a partner in the divine. The temple stands as a testament to Krishna's promise to Sudama, a reminder that he is always there, ready to share in our joys and sorrows.

The story of Sanwaliya Seth is a reflection of the human spirit—its hopes, its struggles, and its unwavering trust in the divine. Whether you come to Mandaphia seeking wealth, healing, or simply a moment of peace, you leave with something greater: a sense of connection to Krishna, the dark lord who fulfills every heart's desire. As the sun sets over the hills of Chittorgarh, casting a golden glow on the temple, the chants of "Jai Sanwaliya Seth!" rise into the sky. The journey to Mandaphia is a journey to Krishna's court, a reminder that with faith, no wish is too big, and no heart too small. And so, the legend of Sanwaliya Seth Mandir lives on, a light of faith for all who seek it.

The Legend of Mehandipur Balaji Dham

The Beginning: A Land Touched by Divinity

In the heart of Rajasthan, where the golden sands of the desert meet the rugged embrace of the Aravali hills, lies a small village called Mehandipur. It's a place that feels like it's caught between worlds—where the air hums with an ancient energy, and the whispers of the divine seem to linger in the breeze. This is the home of Mehandipur Balaji Dham, a sacred temple dedicated to Lord Hanuman, the eternal devotee of Lord Rama, revered here in his child form as Balaji. But this is no ordinary temple. It's a place where miracles unfold, where the battle between good and evil plays out in plain sight, and where the cries of the afflicted are met with the boundless compassion of the divine.

Long ago, in a time when gods and demons walked the earth more freely, Mehandipur was not the bustling pilgrimage site it is today. It was a dense forest, wild and untamed, filled with towering trees, hidden streams, and creatures that roamed under the moon's watchful gaze. The Aravali hills, with their ancient stones, stood as silent sentinels, guarding secrets older than memory itself. The villagers who lived nearby spoke of strange occurrences—whispers in the night, shadows that moved without a source, and a feeling that something powerful, something sacred, was watching over the land.

This is the story of how Mehandipur Balaji Dham came to be—a tale woven from the threads of Hindu scriptures, local legends, and the unshakable faith of millions. It's a story of divine intervention, of a sacred idol that appeared from the earth, and of a temple that became a beacon of hope for those tormented by forces beyond the ordinary. Let me take you back to the beginning, to a time when the gods chose Mehandipur to reveal their presence.

The Divine Dream: The Call of Balaji

It was the 11th century, a time when the world was steeped in both devotion and darkness. The Treta Yuga, the age of Lord Rama, had long passed, but the legacy of his greatest devotee, Hanuman, lived on in the hearts of the faithful. In a small village near Mehandipur, there lived a holy man named Shri Mahant Ji. He was a simple soul, a Brahmin priest who spent his days in prayer, tending to the needs of his village, and seeking the divine in every moment. His heart was pure, his faith unwavering, and his life devoted to serving others.

One night, as the stars glittered above the Aravali hills, Shri Mahant Ji fell into a deep sleep. In his dream, a radiant light filled the sky, and from it emerged three divine figures. The first was a child, glowing with an innocence that belied his immense power. His eyes sparkled with mischief and strength, and in his hand, he held a gada, the mace that symbolized his might. This was Balaji, the child form of Hanuman, the Sankat Mochan, the remover of obstacles. Beside him stood two other figures: Pretraj Sarkar, the stern yet just executioner of the divine court, and Bhairav Kotwal, the fierce commander of Balaji's celestial army, an incarnation of Lord Shiva himself.

The figures spoke to Shri Mahant Ji in a voice that was both thunderous and gentle, like the rumble of a distant storm mixed with the warmth of a mother's lullaby. "This land is sacred," they said. "It is here that we have chosen to manifest, to protect and heal those who suffer. Build a temple in our honor, and we shall reside here, granting solace to the afflicted and strength to the weak."

Shri Mahant Ji awoke with a start, his heart pounding with awe and fear. The vision was so vivid, so real, that he could still feel the warmth of Balaji's presence. He rushed outside, the cool night air brushing against his face, and made his way to the spot he had seen in his dream—a clearing nestled between two hills, where the forest seemed to bow in reverence. There, to his astonishment, he found three idols emerging from the earth, as if the very soil had given birth to them. The idol of Balaji was at the center, a small, radiant figure carved from stone, with a serene smile and eyes that seemed to see into the soul. To his left was Pretraj Sarkar, his form imposing yet protective, and to his right was Bhairav Kotwal, fierce and unyielding, his presence a shield against all evil.

Shri Mahant Ji fell to his knees, tears streaming down his face. He knew this was no ordinary moment. The gods had chosen him, a humble priest, to be their instrument. With the help of the villagers, he began the work of building a temple around these sacred idols. They labored day and night, their hands guided by faith, their hearts filled with devotion. The forest was cleared, stones were laid, and slowly, a temple rose—a simple yet majestic structure that seemed to blend with the hills themselves. Its pillared balconies and arched doorways reflected the Rajput architecture of the time, but there was something otherworldly about it, as if the temple had always been meant to stand there.

Word of the divine appearance spread like wildfire. Villagers from near and far came to see the idols, to offer their prayers, and to seek the blessings of Balaji, Pretraj Sarkar, and Bhairav Kotwal. But this was no ordinary temple. From the very beginning, strange things began to happen. People who were sick or troubled by unseen forces found relief after visiting the temple. Those who felt weighed down by dark energies—ghosts, phantoms, or the effects of black magic—claimed to feel lighter, as if an invisible burden had been lifted. The temple became known as a place of healing, a court where Balaji presided as the divine judge, Pretraj Sarkar as the executioner of justice, and Bhairav Kotwal as the protector who drove away evil.

The Legend of Balaji's Power

The story of Mehandipur Balaji Dham is not just about the temple's origins but also about the countless miracles and legends that have grown around it. One of the most famous tales comes from the early days of the temple, when a man named Gopal arrived in Mehandipur, desperate for help. Gopal was a merchant from a nearby town, once prosperous and happy, but now a shadow of his former self. His family whispered that he was possessed by an evil spirit—a bhoot that had taken hold of him after a business rival cursed him with black magic. Gopal's eyes were wild, his voice no longer his own, and he would scream and thrash at night, terrifying his wife and children.

The local healers had tried everything—mantras, herbs, even tying him with ropes—but nothing worked. In despair, Gopal's wife heard of the new temple in Mehandipur and decided to take him there. The journey was arduous, for Gopal resisted every step, as if the spirit within him knew it was being taken to a place of divine power. When they reached the temple, the air was thick with the scent of incense and the sound of chanting. "Jai Bala!" the devotees cried, their voices rising like a wave.

As Gopal was brought before the idol of Balaji, something miraculous happened. His body began to tremble, and a guttural voice, not his own, cried out, "No! I cannot stay here!" The priests, trained in the temple's rituals, began to chant mantras and sprinkle holy water from the sacred well near the temple. Gopal's wife offered two plates of laddoos, as was the custom, one to seek Balaji's blessings and the other to request his guidance. The priests took the laddoos and placed them in the fire burning before the idol, the flames leaping higher as if fueled by divine energy.

Suddenly, Gopal let out a piercing scream, and his body went limp. The priests continued their chants, their voices steady and powerful. After what seemed like an eternity, Gopal opened his eyes, and for the first time in months, they were clear. He looked at his wife, tears streaming down his face, and said, "I am free." The spirit that had tormented him was gone, banished by the power of Balaji. The crowd erupted in cries of "Jai Hanuman Ki!" and Gopal's wife fell at the feet of the idol, overwhelmed with gratitude.

This was just one of many stories that began to spread. People spoke of Balaji's court, where evil spirits were brought before the divine judge and forced to confess their crimes. Pretraj Sarkar, the executioner, would deliver justice, while Bhairav Kotwal ensured that no malevolent force could linger in the temple's sacred precincts. The temple became a place where the invisible battles of the spirit world were fought and won, where the afflicted found solace, and where the power of Hanuman's devotion to Rama shone like a beacon.

The Rituals: A Dance of Faith and Healing

The Mehandipur Balaji Temple is unlike any other in India. It's not a place of serene worship alone but a battlefield where good triumphs over evil. The rituals here are unique, steeped in tradition and belief, and they form the heart of the temple's mystique. Let me take you through the three main rituals—Durkhasta, Arzi, and Savamani—that define the experience of visiting Mehandipur Balaji.

Durkhasta: The Offering of Intent

When you arrive at Mehandipur, the first thing you notice is the hustle and bustle outside the temple. Small shops line the path, their counters piled high with laddoos, black urad dal, and boiled rice. These are not ordinary offerings but part of the sacred ritual called Durkhasta. If you come to the temple seeking help—whether for a physical ailment, a mental burden, or a spiritual affliction—you begin with Durkhasta.

You purchase two plates of laddoos from one of the shops. These are small, round sweets made of gram flour, sugar, and ghee, simple yet symbolic. As you approach the temple, you hand the plates to the priests standing before the idol of Balaji. The priests, their faces calm yet focused, take a few laddoos and toss them into the fire burning in front of the deity. The flames crackle and rise, as if carrying your prayers to the heavens. The first plate is your way of telling Balaji, "I am here, seeking your blessings." The second is your plea: "Guide me, protect me, heal me."

You repeat this offering before the idols of Pretraj Sarkar and Bhairav Kotwal, completing the circuit of devotion. But the ritual doesn't end there. From the leftover laddoos, you must eat two, a symbolic act of accepting Balaji's blessings. The rest are placed in a container, which you or your family circle around your head seven times in an anticlockwise direction. Then, without looking back, you discard the container. This act is believed to cast away any negative energies clinging to you, ensuring they don't follow you home.

Arzi: The Plea for Justice

If your troubles are deeper—perhaps a persistent illness, a family curse, or the influence of an evil spirit—you move to the next ritual: Arzi. This is a more elaborate offering, a formal plea to the divine court of Balaji. You purchase a set of offerings from the shops outside: 1.25 kilograms of laddoos, 2.25 kilograms of black urad dal, and 4.25 kilograms of boiled rice. These are divided into two containers, one for Pretraj Sarkar and one for Bhairav Kotwal.

As you present the Arzi, the priests chant mantras, their voices rising and falling like the tide. The offerings are placed before the deities, and the atmosphere grows heavy with anticipation. It's said that during this ritual, evil spirits are compelled to appear before Balaji's court. Some devotees claim to hear strange voices or see shadows fleeing the temple. The priests, trained in the art of spiritual warfare, guide the process, ensuring that the divine justice of Balaji prevails.

Savamani: The Vow of Gratitude

The final ritual is Savamani, a promise kept to Balaji. If you've made a wish—perhaps for healing, prosperity, or the resolution of a crisis—you vow to return and offer Savamani once your wish is fulfilled. This ritual is performed only on Tuesdays and Saturdays, the days sacred to Hanuman. Savamani involves offering halwa puri, a rich dish of sweetened semolina and fried bread, to the deities. The temple trust prepares the bhog, which is first offered to Balaji and then distributed among the devotees.

Savamani is a moment of celebration, a way to thank Balaji for his grace. But it comes with a condition: you must return to the temple to fulfill your vow. To break this promise is to invite misfortune, for Balaji's blessings are not to be taken lightly.

The Rules of the Temple

The rituals of Mehandipur Balaji come with strict rules, born of centuries of tradition and belief. You must not eat or drink anything inside the temple premises, for fear that an evil spirit might taint the food. You must not touch or speak to strangers, as they could be possessed, and their affliction could pass to you. Photography is forbidden, as capturing the temple's image might trap its sacred energy. And most importantly, when you leave the temple, you must not look back, lest an evil spirit follows you out.

These rules may seem strange to outsiders, but to the devotees who flock to Mehandipur, they are a small price to pay for the chance to stand in Balaji's presence. The temple is a place of power, and
with power comes responsibility.

The Court of Balaji: A Spiritual Battlefield

The Mehandipur Balaji Temple is often described as a divine court, where Balaji presides as the judge, Pretraj Sarkar as the executioner, and Bhairav Kotwal as the protector. This imagery comes from the belief that the temple is a place where evil spirits are brought to justice. Devotees speak of the "peshi," or court hearing, where possessed individuals are presented before Balaji's idol. The priests chant mantras, sprinkle holy water, and burn offerings, creating an atmosphere charged with spiritual energy.

One of the most striking sights in the temple is the Hajuri Aarti, held every evening around 5 or 6 p.m. During this ritual, those believed to be possessed are brought before the idol of Balaji. The air fills with the sound of chanting—"Jai Bala! Jai Hanuman Ki!"—and the possessed often react dramatically. Some scream, others thrash, and some speak in voices that seem to come from another world. The priests remain calm, their faith unshaken, guiding the afflicted through the ritual until the evil spirit is driven out.

One story tells of a young woman named Urmilla, whose case was studied by scholars. Urmilla, an 18-year-old from a nearby village, began acting strangely after her marriage. She would speak in a hoarse voice, claiming to know things only a long-dead relative could know. Her family, terrified, brought her to Mehandipur. During the Hajuri Aarti, Urmilla's body shook violently, and a voice not her own cried out, begging for mercy. The priests chanted tirelessly, and after hours of struggle, Urmilla collapsed, exhausted but free. When she awoke, she was herself again, her eyes filled with gratitude for Balaji's grace.

Such stories are common at Mehandipur. The temple is a place where the boundaries between the physical and spiritual worlds blur, where the power of faith confronts the forces of darkness. For many, it's a last resort, a place to turn when all else fails. And for those who leave healed, it's a testament to the enduring power of Hanuman, the Sankat Mochan.

The Legends of Hanuman and Mehandipur

To understand the significance of Mehandipur Balaji, we must look to the broader tapestry of Hindu mythology, particularly the stories of Hanuman from the Ramayana. Hanuman, the monkey god, is one of the most beloved figures in Hinduism. He is the epitome of devotion, strength, and loyalty, serving as Lord Rama's most trusted companion in the epic battle against Ravana.

In the Ramayana, Hanuman's exploits are legendary. He leapt across the ocean to find Sita, set fire to Lanka with his burning tail, and carried an entire mountain to bring the Sanjeevani herb to save Lakshmana's life. But at Mehandipur, Hanuman is worshipped in his child form, Balaji, a symbol of innocence and boundless power. This child form is significant, for it represents Hanuman's early feats, such as his attempt to swallow the sun, mistaking it for a ripe fruit. Even as a child, Hanuman was unstoppable, a force of divine energy that could not be contained.

The connection between Hanuman and Mehandipur is rooted in the belief that his power transcends time. The Ramayana tells us that Hanuman is immortal, blessed by Rama to remain on earth as long as his name is chanted. At Mehandipur, devotees believe that Hanuman chose this sacred spot to manifest his presence, to continue his work of protecting the faithful and vanquishing evil.

One local legend ties Mehandipur to the Ramayana itself. It's said that during Rama's exile, Hanuman passed through the Aravali hills while searching for Sita. The energy of his

presence lingered in the land, imbuing it with divine power. When the time came for a temple to be built, Hanuman chose Mehandipur as the place where his child form would reside, a beacon of hope for those in
need.

Another legend speaks of a demon named Ghata Asura, a malevolent spirit who tormented the people of the region long ago. The villagers, desperate for relief, prayed to the gods for help. Hanuman, in his child form, appeared before them, his small frame radiating immense power. With a single swing of his gada, he vanquished the demon, freeing the land from its curse. The idol of Balaji at Mehandipur is said to mark the spot where this battle took place, a reminder of Hanuman's eternal vigilance.

The Beliefs: A Tapestry of Faith

The Mehandipur Balaji Temple is more than a physical place; it's a symbol of hope, faith, and the triumph of good over evil. The beliefs surrounding the temple are deeply rooted in Hindu spirituality, but they also reflect the unique cultural and historical context of Rajasthan.

One of the core beliefs is that Balaji has the power to heal not just physical ailments but spiritual ones as well. Devotees come to Mehandipur seeking relief from "pret badha" (ghostly afflictions), "bhoot-pret" (evil spirits), and "kala jadu" (black magic). These are not just superstitions but part of a worldview that acknowledges the existence of unseen forces. In Hindu cosmology, the universe is populated by gods, demons, and spirits, and Mehandipur is seen as a place where these forces are brought into balance.

Another belief is that the temple operates as a divine court, where Balaji presides over the fate of evil spirits. Pretraj Sarkar, the executioner, is believed to punish those spirits that harm the innocent, while Bhairav Kotwal ensures that no malevolent force can linger in the temple's sacred space. This imagery resonates deeply with devotees, who see the temple as a place of justice and protection.

The temple is also associated with the concept of "Sankat Mochan," a title often given to Hanuman. It means "the remover of obstacles," and at Mehandipur, this aspect of Hanuman is paramount. Whether it's a physical illness, a mental struggle, or a spiritual affliction, devotees believe that Balaji can remove any obstacle, no matter how insurmountable it seems.

One of the most intriguing beliefs is the prohibition against taking prasad home. Unlike other temples, where prasad is a sacred offering to be shared with family, at Mehandipur, the prasad—whether laddoos or other offerings—must be consumed or discarded at the temple. This stems from the belief that the prasad absorbs negative energies during the rituals, and taking it home could bring those energies with it. Devotees are also warned not to look back as they leave the temple, for fear that an evil spirit might follow them.

The Modern Pilgrimage: A Journey of Faith

Today, Mehandipur Balaji Dham is one of the most visited pilgrimage sites in India, drawing thousands of devotees every day, especially on Tuesdays and Saturdays, when Hanuman's power is believed to be at its peak. The temple is located in the Dausa district of Rajasthan, about 120 kilometers from Jaipur and 300 kilometers from Delhi. It's accessible by road, with buses and taxis ferrying pilgrims from nearby cities. The nearest railway stations are in Dausa, Bandikui, and Hindaun City, making it a convenient destination for those traveling by train.

The temple itself is a blend of simplicity and grandeur. Its architecture reflects the Rajput style, with pillared balconies and intricately carved doorways. The idols of Balaji, Pretraj Sarkar, and Bhairav Kotwal are housed in separate sanctums, each radiating a distinct energy. The temple complex is surrounded by dharamshalas (guesthouses) that offer lodging and meals for pilgrims, many of whom stay for days or even weeks to complete their rituals.

The atmosphere at Mehandipur is unlike any other temple. The air is thick with the scent of incense, the sound of chanting, and the cries of those seeking relief. It's a place of contrasts—serene yet intense, sacred yet eerie. For some, it's a place of profound peace; for others, it's a battlefield where the forces of good and evil clash. But for all who come, it's a place of hope, a reminder that no matter how dark the night, the light of Balaji's grace will always shine through.

The Critics: Faith Meets Skepticism

Not everyone believes in the miracles of Mehandipur Balaji. Some scholars and skeptics argue that the temple's reputation for exorcism is rooted in cultural and psychological factors rather than supernatural ones. They point to the power of suggestion, the placebo effect, and the role of ritual in addressing mental health issues.

But for the devotees who flock to Mehandipur, these explanations matter little. To them, the temple is a place of divine intervention, where Balaji's power transcends science and logic. The debate between faith and skepticism is as old as time, and at Mehandipur, it's a reminder that truth often lies in the eye of the beholder.

The Legacy: A Beacon of Hope

This is a place where the impossible becomes possible, where the afflicted find healing, and where the divine touches the human. The temple stands as a testament to the enduring power of Hanuman, the Sankat Mochan, whose devotion to Rama inspires millions to this day.

The story of Mehandipur Balaji is not just a tale of a temple but a reflection of the human spirit—its struggles, its hopes, and its unyielding faith in the face of darkness. Whether you come to Mehandipur seeking healing, guidance, or simply a glimpse of the divine, you leave with something greater: a sense of connection to a power larger than yourself, a power that has guided humanity through the ages.

As the sun sets over the Aravali hills, casting a golden glow over the temple, the chants of "Jai Bala!" rise into the sky. The journey to Mehandipur is a journey into the heart of faith, a reminder that no matter how great the obstacle, Balaji's grace is greater still. And so, the legend of Mehandipur Balaji Dham lives on, a beacon of hope for all who seek it.

Lord Jagannath

Imagine standing on the shores of Puri, Odisha, where the waves of the Bay of Bengal whisper ancient tales. The salty breeze carries the chants of devotees, and in the heart of this sacred city stands the majestic Jagannath Temple, home to Lord Jagannath, the "Lord of the Universe." His name, derived from the Sanskrit words *Jagat* (world) and *Natha* (lord), speaks of his boundless presence. To millions, he is more than a deity; he is a friend, a protector, and a symbol of unity. His story is a tapestry woven from tribal roots, Vedic traditions, and divine mysteries.

The Origins: A Divine Beginning Rooted in Mystery

Long before temples rose and priests chanted mantras, Lord Jagannath was a presence in the forests of Odisha. The story begins with the Sabara tribe, a forest-dwelling community who worshipped a deity called Neelamadhava, a blue stone idol believed to be a manifestation of Lord Vishnu. This tribal deity, simple yet sacred, was revered in a cave hidden deep in the Nilachala (Blue Mountain) region of Puri. The Sabaras, led by their chief Vishwavasu, offered their devotion to this deity with rituals that were raw, heartfelt, and untouched by the complexities of organized religion.

This tribal connection is the first thread in Jagannath's story. Unlike the polished stone or metal idols of other Hindu temples, Jagannath's wooden form, carved from neem wood, hints at these ancient roots. The Sabaras worshipped wooden poles, a practice that echoes in the unique, unfinished appearance of Jagannath's idol—large round eyes, a broad smile, and no hands or legs. This form, so different from traditional Hindu iconography, tells us that Jagannath is a deity who transcends convention, embracing all who come to him, regardless of caste or creed.

But how did this tribal deity become the Lord of the Universe? The answer lies in a divine dream and a king named Indradyumna. According to the *Skanda Purana* and local legends recorded in the *Madala Panji* (the temple chronicles of Puri), Indradyumna, a king of the Malava region, was a devout follower of Lord Vishnu. One night, Vishnu appeared in his dream, revealing the existence of Neelamadhava in the forests of Odisha. The king's heart burned with a longing to see this deity and build a temple to honor him. He sent his trusted priest, Vidyapati, to find this sacred idol.

Vidyapati's journey was not easy. The Sabaras guarded Neelamadhava fiercely, and Vishwavasu, the tribal chief, was reluctant to share his deity with outsiders. But Vidyapati, driven by devotion and aided by a love story with Vishwavasu's daughter Lalita, gained the chief's trust. He learned of the secret cave where Neelamadhava was worshipped. When Indradyumna arrived, however, the idol mysteriously vanished, leaving the king heartbroken. Vishnu, moved by Indradyumna's devotion, spoke to him again, instructing him to find a sacred log floating in the ocean. This log, said to be from a divine neem tree from the spiritual realm of Svetadvipa, would become the foundation for Jagannath's idol.

The king found the log, but no one could move it. It was too heavy, too sacred. Once again, the Sabaras came to the rescue. A descendant of Vishwavasu, with his tribal strength and connection to the deity, lifted the log with ease. The divine architect Vishwakarma, disguised as an old carpenter, appeared to carve the idols of Jagannath, his brother Balabhadra, and sister Subhadra. He worked in seclusion, with one condition: no one could disturb him. But curiosity got the better of Indradyumna and his queen, Gundicha. They opened the door before the work was complete, and Vishwakarma vanished, leaving the idols unfinished—without hands, legs, or refined features. A divine voice reassured the king that these forms were perfect, a symbol of Jagannath's universal love and accessibility. Thus, the deities were installed in a grand temple, and Jagannath's worship began.

This story, found in texts like the *Skanda Purana* and *Brahma Purana*, blends tribal simplicity with Vedic grandeur. It tells us

that Jagannath is not just a Hindu god but a deity who bridges worlds—tribal and Vedic, human and divine. The unfinished idols, with their large, compassionate eyes, seem to say, "I am here for everyone, in whatever form you need me to be."

From Tribal Deity to Universal Lord

While the legend of Indradyumna gives Jagannath a mythical origin, history tells us how he grew into a cultural and spiritual icon. The Jagannath Temple in Puri, as we know it today, was built in the 12th century by King Anantavarman Chodaganga Deva of the Eastern Ganga dynasty. This king, originally a Shaivite, embraced Vaishnavism under the influence of the saint Ramanuja, and his devotion to Jagannath helped transform the deity from a local figure to a central pillar of Odisha's identity. The temple, a masterpiece of Kalinga architecture with its towering spire, became a symbol of spiritual and political power.

But Jagannath's history goes deeper. Some scholars point to hymn 10.155.3 of the *Rigveda*, which mentions a "Daru" (wooden log) wandering in the sea, as a possible reference to Jagannath's origins. While this interpretation is debated, it suggests that the concept of a deity emerging from wood has ancient roots. Others argue that Jagannath's worship predates Vedic traditions, rooted in the tribal practices of Odisha's indigenous communities. The Daitapatis, temple servitors who claim descent from the Sabaras, still play a key role in rituals, a living link to this tribal past.

Over centuries, Jagannath's cult absorbed influences from Jainism, Buddhism, and Tantric traditions. The *Kalika Purana* describes Jagannath as a Tantric deity, with yantras (mystical diagrams) engraved on the *Ratnavedi* (the platform where the deities are placed). Some Buddhists believe that Jagannath's idol contains a relic of the Buddha, possibly a tooth from Kushinagar, linking him to Buddhist traditions. Jain influences are seen in the deity's non-caste-based worship and the symbolism of the trinity—Jagannath as *sunya* (void), Subhadra as creative energy, and Balabhadra as the phenomenal universe.

This syncretism is Jagannath's strength. He is Vishnu to Vaishnavas, Krishna to Krishnaites, Bhairava to Shaivas, and even a symbol of the Buddha or a Jain Tirthankara to others. The *Ramayana* mentions Jagannath as the deity of Lord Rama's Ikshvaku clan, and the *Mahabharata* connects him to King Indradyumna's Ashvamedha Yajna. Poets like Sarala Das, in his 15th-century *Odia Mahabharata*, portray Jagannath as both Krishna and the Buddha, reflecting Odisha's ability to embrace diverse faiths.

The Gajapati kings, who ruled Odisha as Jagannath's earthly representatives, played a crucial role in this evolution. They saw themselves as the deity's first servants (*chalanti pratima*), performing rituals like *Chera Pahara*, where the king sweeps the chariots during the Rath Yatra. This act symbolizes humility, showing that even the mightiest ruler is equal before Jagannath. The temple's lack of caste distinctions—where all devotees can enter and eat the *Mahaprasad* (sacred food offering)—further cements Jagannath's universal appeal.

A God for All

At the heart of Jagannath's worship is the belief that he is *Purushottama*, the Supreme Being who transcends all boundaries. To Vaishnavas, he is Krishna, the playful yet profound deity of the *Bhagavad Gita*. To others, he is Vishnu, the preserver of the universe, or even a fierce form of Shiva. His black complexion, like Krishna's, represents the common farmer tanned by the sun, while Balabhadra's fair skin symbolizes royalty, and Subhadra's yellow hue reflects the warmth of the hearth. Together, they embody humanity in all its diversity.

Jagannath's devotees believe he is compassionate and accessible.

Stories abound of him taking on the suffering of his devotees, even falling ill for them. His large, round eyes are said to see every heart, and his lack of hands and legs symbolizes that he needs no physical form to act—he works through the devotion of his followers. The *Mahaprasad*, offered first to Goddess Vimala in the temple complex, is a sacred bond between Jagannath and his devotees, shared by all without distinction.

Another key belief is Jagannath's omnipresence. The *Skanda Purana* calls him *Darubrahma*, the Supreme

Brahman in wooden form. His idol, though simple, is believed to contain a mystical substance called *Brahma*, possibly a relic or a sacred stone, transferred during the *Navakalebara* ritual. This belief underscores his eternal nature, unchanging even as his wooden form is renewed every 12 to 19 years.

Jagannath's worship also reflects a deep connection to nature. The neem wood of his idols, the banyan tree near which he first appeared, and the ocean that brought his sacred log all tie him to the natural world. This resonates with tribal traditions of tree and wood worship, making Jagannath a deity who bridges the human and natural realms.

The beauty of Lord Jagannath lies not just in his divine form but in the stories that surround him. These tales, passed down through generations, are like pearls strung together, each one shining with devotion, humor, and wisdom. They come from scriptures like the *Skanda Purana*, *Brahma Purana*, and *Sarala Mahabharata*, as well as oral traditions kept alive by the people of Odisha. Let's dive into some of the most beloved stories and myths that make Jagannath a living deity in the hearts of millions.

The Legend of King Indradyumna and the Divine Log

In the *Skanda Purana*, Indradyumna is described as a king of the Satya Yuga, a golden age of truth and prosperity. His heart ached to see Lord Vishnu face-to-face, a desire so pure that Vishnu himself took notice. In a dream, the Lord revealed the existence of Neelamadhava, worshipped by the Sabara tribe in Odisha. Indradyumna sent Vidyapati, his Brahmin priest, to find this deity. Vidyapati, through cunning and love, won over Vishwavasu and saw the blue idol in its secret cave. But when Indradyumna arrived, the idol vanished, testing his faith.

Heartbroken but undeterred, the king fasted and prayed. Vishnu appeared again, guiding him to a log floating in the sea, glowing with divine energy. This was no ordinary wood—it was said to be from a *kalpa-vriksha*, a wish-fulfilling tree from the spiritual realm. The king's army couldn't move it, but a Sabara descendant of Vishwavasu lifted it effortlessly, proving the deity's connection to the tribal people. Vishwakarma, the divine architect, began carving the idols, but when Indradyumna and Queen Gundicha peeked too soon, the work stopped. The unfinished idols—Jagannath, Balabhadra, Subhadra, and the Sudarshana Chakra—were installed in a grand temple, consecrated by Lord Brahma himself. This story teaches us that devotion, even when tested, leads to divine grace.

The Tale of Bandhu Mohanty: Loyalty Rewarded

One of the most heartwarming stories is that of Bandhu Mohanty, a poor devotee whose loyalty touched Jagannath's heart. Bandhu lived near the Puri temple and served it humbly, carrying water for the rituals despite his poverty. One day, he faced a crisis—his family had no food, and he had nothing to offer. In despair, he prayed to Jagannath, who appeared at his doorstep disguised as a stranger, asking for food. Bandhu, though starving, offered his last scraps. Moved by his selflessness, Jagannath revealed himself and blessed Bandhu with prosperity. This tale, popular in Odisha, shows that Jagannath values the purity of the heart over wealth or status.

The Devotion of Salabega: A Muslim's Love for Jagannath

Salabega, born in 1592 to a Muslim warrior and a Hindu mother, is one of Jagannath's most famous devotees. Raised as a Muslim, he was drawn to Jagannath's temple in Puri after hearing of its universal appeal. But as a non-Hindu, he was barred from entering. Undeterred, Salabega composed devotional songs from outside the temple, pouring his heart into verses that are still sung today. During one Rath Yatra, he fell ill and couldn't attend. Legend says Jagannath's chariot miraculously stopped near Salabega's home, allowing him to see the Lord. This story reflects Jagannath's non-sectarian nature, embracing devotees of all faiths.

The Kanchi Conquest: Jagannath's Playful Victory

The *Kanchi-Kaveri* legend is a delightful tale of divine mischief. In the 15th century, the Gajapati king of Puri,

Purushottama Deva, sought to marry the princess of Kanchi. The Kanchi king, insulted by the Gajapati's act of sweeping Jagannath's chariot during Rath Yatra (mistaking it for lowliness), refused the alliance. Enraged, Purushottama Deva waged war but was defeated. He prayed to Jagannath, who, along with Balabhadra, rode to battle on horseback, disguised as soldiers. They defeated the Kanchi army, and Jagannath playfully demanded a sweet dish, *rasgulla*, as tribute. The princess, awed by Jagannath's power, married the Gajapati, and the *rasgulla* became a beloved offering in Puri. This story shows Jagannath as a protector who fights for his devotees, with a touch of humor.

The Mystery of the Brahma: A Buddhist Connection?

A fascinating myth surrounds the *Brahma*, a sacred substance inside Jagannath's idol. Some Buddhists believe it is a tooth relic of Gautama Buddha, brought from Kushinagar to Puri. The *Skanda Purana* hints that Jagannath's idol contains Krishna's ashes, a practice rare in Hinduism but common in Buddhism, where relics are revered. During the *Navakalebara* ritual, this *Brahma* is transferred to the new idol in a secret ceremony, adding to the deity's mystique. Whether Hindu or Buddhist, this belief underscores Jagannath's ability to unite diverse faiths.

Jayadeva's Devotion: The Gita Govinda

The 12th-century poet Jayadeva, author of the *Gita Govinda*, was a devoted follower of Jagannath. Legend says he wanted to offer his masterpiece, a poetic celebration of Krishna's love for Radha, to Jagannath by inscribing it on a garment. Doubting his work, he hesitated, but Jagannath himself appeared in a dream, urging him to complete it. The verses were offered at the temple, and today, *Gita Govinda* is sung during Jagannath's rituals, a testament to the deity's patronage of art and devotion.

Lord Jagannath is more than a deity; he is a way of life, a symbol of unity, and a beacon of hope. His significance lies in his ability to bring people together, transcending barriers of caste, religion, and status. In this final part, we'll explore the rituals that keep his worship alive, the modern-day vibrancy of his cult, and why Jagannath remains relevant in today's world.

Significance: A Universal Symbol of Love

Jagannath's greatest significance is his inclusivity. The temple's doors are open to all, and the *Mahaprasad* is shared without discrimination. This reflects the belief that Jagannath is the Lord of all humanity, not just Hindus. His worship blends tribal, Vedic, Buddhist, Jain, and Tantric elements, making him a symbol of India's cultural syncretism. The *Chera Pahara* ritual, where the Gajapati king sweeps the chariots, reminds us that before Jagannath, all are equal.

Jagannath also represents resilience. Despite invasions and attempts to plunder the Puri temple, his worship has endured, protected by the Gajapati kings and devotees. The term "juggernaut," derived from Jagannath, entered English to describe an unstoppable force, a testament to his enduring power.

Rituals: A Living Tradition

The Jagannath Temple is a hub of rituals, each steeped in meaning. Daily offerings, or *bhogas*, are made six times a day, from the morning *Gopala Vallabha Bhoga* (breakfast) to the *Bada Singhara Bhoga* (night offering). The *Mahaprasad*, cooked in earthen pots over a wood fire, is first offered to Goddess Vimala, making it uniquely sacred.

The *Rath Yatra*, held annually in June or July (on July 27, 2025, per recent sources), is the most famous ritual. Jagannath, Balabhadra, and Subhadra are placed on massive wooden chariots and taken to the Gundicha Temple, believed to be their aunt's home. The procession, attended by millions, symbolizes Jagannath's journey to meet his devotees. The *Chera Pahara* ritual, where the Gajapati king sweeps the chariots, is a highlight, emphasizing humility.

The *Navakalebara* ritual, performed every 12 to 19 years, is a profound ceremony. New idols are carved from sacred neem trees, and the *Brahma* is transferred in a secret ritual led by the Daitapatis. This symbolizes the cycle of life, death, and rebirth, reminding devotees of Jagannath's eternal presence.

The *Snana Purnima*, where the deities are bathed with Ascetic water, is another vibrant ritual. After the bath, Jagannath takes on the *Hati Vesha* (elephant attire), symbolizing Ganesha's blessings. These rituals, rooted in ancient texts like the *Oddiyana Tantras*, blend tribal and Vedic traditions, making them uniquely inclusive.

Modern-Day Scene: Jagannath in Today's World

Today, Jagannath's worship thrives not just in Puri but globally. The Rath Yatra is celebrated in cities worldwide, from New York to London, thanks to the efforts of ISKCON and other devotees. In 2025, Puri's Rath Yatra is expected to draw millions, with vibrant processions, devotional songs, and *Mahaprasad* distribution. Social media posts on X reflect the excitement, with devotees sharing stories and images of the festival's grandeur.

The temple remains a cultural hub, inspiring art forms like Pattachitra paintings and Odissi dance, both of which depict Jagannath's stories. Online platforms like Svastika.in and Poojn.in offer devotees a way to connect, selling traditional idols and puja items. Jagannath's teachings of love, equality, and devotion resonate in a world often divided by differences, making his message timeless.

Lord Jagannath's story is a journey from a tribal deity to a universal symbol of love and unity. His origins in the forests of Odisha, his divine manifestation through King Indradyumna, and his evolution through history show a deity who embraces all. His stories—of Bandhu Mohanty's loyalty, Salabega's devotion, and the Kanchi conquest—reveal a god who is playful, compassionate, and accessible. His rituals, from the grand Rath Yatra to the sacred Navakalebara, keep his presence alive, while his modern-day worship shows his relevance in a globalized world.

Jagannath teaches us that divinity is not confined to temples or rituals but lives in the heart of every devotee. Whether you see him as Krishna, Vishnu, or a tribal god, his message is clear: love, equality, and faith can unite us all. As you stand before his smiling idol, with its large, all-seeing eyes, you feel his promise—to be with you, always, as the Lord of the Universe.

Ending Note

As you turn the final page of this book, I offer you my deepest gratitude for walking alongside me on this spiritual and mythological journey. Each story you've read is not just a tale from the past, but a living essence of faith, devotion, and divine energy that still flows through the heart of India today.

Whether it was the battlefield where Lord Murugan's valor shone, the mystical depths of Patala ruled by Ahiravana, or the sacred soil of Khatu and Salasar where countless devotees surrender their pain—these narratives carry with them timeless wisdom. They remind us that the divine is not confined to the heavens; it is ever-present in our daily struggles, in our moments of doubt, in our celebrations, and most importantly, in our faith.

These stories are not meant to be finished and forgotten. They are seeds—seeds of reflection, humility, strength, and devotion. I hope some part of this book stayed with you, touched your soul, and reminded you of the invisible thread that connects us all to something greater, kinder, and eternal.

But this journey is far from over.

India's spiritual landscape is vast and deeply layered. There are still many more temples to visit, deities to meet, and untold stories waiting patiently in the folds of time. I am already working on **Part 2**, where we will continue this sacred journey with new legends, lesser-known temples, and deeper insights into the mysteries of dharma and divinity.

So until we meet again in the next volume, may your path be blessed with light, may your faith grow stronger, and may the stories you've read here continue to guide and protect you.

Thank you for trusting me with your time and heart.

With reverence and love,

Rajnish Kumar

https://sanskarsarovar.blogspot.com/

puruji.rk@gmail.com

+91-9855103353

YouTube

Spotify

www.ingramcontent.com/pod-product-compliance
Ingram Content Group UK Ltd.
Pitfield, Milton Keynes, MK11 3LW, UK
UKHW021402190726
13845UKWH00028B/823

9 789334 351071